Schreiben ohne Leiden!

PETER LUPSON

Also available from Stanley Thornes (Publishers) Ltd

EVERYDAY GERMAN IDIOMS
> J.P. Lupson

EINFACH TOLL!
> Patricia M. Smith
> PROJECT COORDINATOR: Philip Wood

LOS GEHT'S!
> Hartmut Aufderstraße et al.
> UK PROJECT COORDINATOR: J.P. Lupson

AINSI VA LA FRANCE
> Ross Steele and Jacqueline Gaillard

FRENCH VERBS AND ESSENTIALS OF GRAMMAR
> Simone Oudot

GUIDE TO CORRESPONDENCE IN FRENCH
> Simone Oudot

TABLEAUX CULTURELS
> J Suzanne Ravise

Schreiben ohne Leiden!

PETER LUPSON M.A. Dip. Ed. F. Coll. P.

HEAD OF MODERN LANGUAGES
WEATHERHEAD HIGH SCHOOL, WALLASEY

STANLEY THORNES (PUBLISHERS) LTD

First published in 1985 by
Stanley Thornes (Publishers) Ltd
Old Station Drive, Leckhampton,
CHELTENHAM GL53 0DN

British Library Cataloguing in Publication Data
Lupson, J.P.
Schreiben ohne Leiden!
1. German language – Composition and exercises
I. Title
808'.0431'076   PF3425
ISBN 0–85950–248–1

Typeset in Raleigh 11/12½
by Factel Ltd., Cheltenham
Printed and bound in Great Britain by The Bath Press, Avon

For Evelyn, Karen and Michael

Acknowledgements

I would like to record my gratitude to my wife, Evelyn, for the ideas on which many of the picture compositions are based, and for the time she spent on the preliminary artwork for these compositions.

I would also like to express my gratitude to Gabriele Zagel for typing my manuscript and for carefully checking the German content, and to my former pupils at Kingsway High School, Chester – Nicola Evans, Martin Jones, Paul Jones, Caroline Pugh, Ian Pugh, Rachael Williams and Stephen Woolnough – for the care and patience with which they copied out the model letters.

The following examination boards have kindly allowed the use of questions from their papers: Oxford and Cambridge School Examinations Board; South Western Examinations Board; Welsh Joint Education Committee; Yorkshire Regional Examinations Board.

Guidance notes for the picture compositions in question have been developed by the author, and should not in any sense be taken as specifically endorsed by the examination boards.

Contents

NOTES FOR TEACHERS

In my experience as an examiner at Certificate level, I have found that many candidates are not really sure about how to approach essay and letter writing tasks. Some attempt to write imaginatively, but at the expense of grammatical accuracy; whilst others limit themselves to simplistic language structures and unimaginative content. Reconciling authentic and appropriate use of language with imaginative and relevant content involves some very real difficulties, and this book sets out to give pupils step by step guidance in developing the necessary skills.

The book covers the writing tasks which are common to most Certificate examinations boards. For each particular kind of writing, it provides:

● an explanation of the basic principles appropriate to the task
● a model showing how these principles are applied
● guided practice in the tasks themselves

Part One discusses important basic aspects of writing in German. Part Two deals specifically with different kinds of essay writing, including Picture Composition. Part Three deals with letter writing. Part Four provides a 'language resource bank' which can be drawn from when tackling the practical work included in Parts Two and Three. (Specific suggestions for introducing particular items from the resource bank are made in each writing exercise.)

Part One
WRITING IN GERMAN

1

Writing in German – Points to Consider

1) THE ESSENTIALS OF A COMPOSITION

The three most important things to consider when preparing an essay or a letter are:

a) CONTENT – what you are going to write about;

b) STRUCTURE – how you are going to organise and present your ideas;

c) STYLE – the kind of language you are going to use to express your ideas.

2) THE RÔLE OF IMAGINATION

Although a lively imagination will be a great help in writing interestingly in German, it is not the most important thing an examiner is looking for. What really matters is: How accurately and authentically can you write German? Even the most exciting story is difficult to enjoy if the reader is trying to make sense of awkward sentence constructions and wrong use of vocabulary.

3) THINKING IN GERMAN

Before you put pen to paper, try to work out in German what you want to say. If you find that you are struggling for the words you need to express your ideas, think of something else to say, for which you **do** have the necesssary vocabulary. Always start from what you **know** is correct German, and build your content around it. Don't be tempted to translate from English. It may be helpful to think of composition tasks as an invitation to you to show off what you know, rather than as a trap designed to reveal what you don't know!

1) ACHIEVING A SMOOTH FLOW

It is important that your composition should flow smoothly. Jerky accounts are usually uninteresting to read. You can achieve a smooth flow in two ways.

a) TIME LINKS – These will make clear **how far apart in time** actions and events are. Useful expressions that you can use are:

Einige Minuten später	–	A few minutes later
Es dauerte einige Zeit, bis . . .	–	It took some time until . . .
Früh am nächsten Morgen	–	Early next morning
Kurz danach	–	Shortly after

b) EXPLANATION LINKS – Always try to explain how actions, events and circumstances are **related** to each other. Conjunctions such as *als* = when; *da* = since, as; *nachdem* = after; and *weil* = because, are invaluable in this respect. Here are two examples of use.

> *Nachdem er auf die Uhr gesehen hatte, lief Erich aus dem Haus.*
> (After he had looked at the time Erich ran out of the house.)

> *Weil es heftig zu regnen begann, verließen sie den Strand.*
> (Because it began to rain heavily they left the beach.)

N.B. Notice the position of the verb at the end of a clause introduced by conjunctions such as *als, da, nachdem, weil.*

2) USE OF LANGUAGE

It is the kind of language you decide to use that provides the examiner with the material he needs to assess your command of German. Since most marks in composition tasks are awarded for language, your choice of language is very important because it will reveal your **command of grammar** and your **range of vocabulary**.

GRAMMAR

There are three areas in particular in which a candidate can demonstrate his or her command of German grammar.

a) USE OF CASES – The commonness of prepositions, verbs followed by the dative (*geben, sagen,* etc.) and the masculine object (*den, einen, ihn,* etc.) makes it extremely difficult to avoid case changes in German. You will find it well worthwhile to take the time to learn the cases thoroughly, as you will need to show you know them in your composition tasks. Basic mistakes in this area are still one of the commonest causes of failed examinations.

b) USE OF VERBS — <u>Tenses</u> Try to show that you have mastered a variety of tenses. For essay tasks in which you are required to write in the past tense, you should use the **simple past tense** (imperfect) for telling a story, but the **perfect tense** in conversation, e.g.

> *„Was hast du denn angestellt?" verlangte sein Vater ärgerlich.*
> ("What have you been up to?" his father demanded angrily.)

When using the perfect tense, try to include verbs with *sein* as well as verbs with *haben*, e.g.

> *„Was ist denn passiert?" fragte sein Vater erschrocken.*
> ("What has happened?", his father asked in alarm.)

You should also use the **pluperfect tense** when possible, e.g.

> *Obgleich sie den Einbruch nicht gesehen hatte, wußte sie, wer der Dieb war.*
> (Although she hadn't seen the burglary, she knew who the thief was.)

By introducing conversation, you can easily include the **future tense**, e.g.

> *„Ich werde dich morgen um halb acht anrufen", sagte Ilse.*
> ("I shall phone you tomorrow at 7.30," said Ilse.)

<u>Variety of verb types</u> There are a handful of verbs that are common knowledge to all students of German. To show that you are not limited to these, try to include as much variety as you can in the types of verbs that you use. In addition to familiar strong and weak verbs, use **separable verbs**, e.g.

> *Der Zug <u>fuhr</u> in den Bahnhof <u>ein</u>* — The train entered the station
> *Sie <u>ging</u> schnell an ihm <u>vorbei</u>* — She quickly went past him

and **impersonal verbs** such as *gefallen* and *gelingen*, e.g.

> *„Es gefällt mir hier nicht", sagte Inge. „Ich finde es langweilig."*
> ("I don't like it here", said Inge. "I think it's boring.")

> *Es gelang ihm endlich, vom Baum herunterzukommen.*
> (He finally succeeded in getting down from the tree.)

c) SENTENCE STRUCTURE — A collection of simple sentences following the pattern subject–verb–object will result in a monotonous piece of writing. You should try to show your mastery of word order by writing sentences in which the position of the verb is varied. The following examples show how sentence structure reveals different levels of mastery of German.

Level 1: *Herr Müller trägt heute einen Mantel. Es ist sehr kalt.*

Level 2: *Heute trägt Herr Müller einen Mantel. Es ist sehr kalt.*
(Inversion of subject and verb in the main clause.)

Level 3: *Heute trägt Herr Müller einen Mantel, weil es sehr kalt ist.*
(Introduction of a subordinate clause.)

Level 4: *Weil es sehr kalt ist, trägt Herr Müller heute einen Mantel.*
(Subordinate clause preceding main clause.)

In terms of content there is not much difference between the sentences in Levels 1 and 4. There is, however, a great difference in terms of complexity of sentence structure. You can see now why more marks are awarded for language than for content.

To demonstrate further your command of word order, show that you know how to use the Time–Manner–Place or WANN?–WIE?–WO? rule, e.g. *Ilse fuhr gestern mit der Bahn nach Hause.*

	Time	Manner	Place
	WANN?	WIE?	WO?

VOCABULARY

The style of your composition will be improved if your vocabulary is not limited to a narrow range, and if you can use idioms effectively.

a) RANGE

(i) Almost all students of German can use words like *groß, klein, Baum* and *Vogel*. To make your composition more interesting try to be as **precise** as possible. You can replace the above, for instance, with *riesig* (huge), *winzig* (tiny), *Eiche* (oak tree) and *Amsel* (blackbird) respectively.

(ii) After using direct speech, do not limit yourself to bald statements like *'antwortete Hans.'* It would be far more effective to state how Hans answered, e.g. *ärgerlich* — annoyed, *empört* — enraged, *ängstlich* — anxiously, *vergnügt* — pleased.

(iii) In describing someone's actions, try to use **adverbs** wherever possible. Things can be done hastily (*hastig*), skilfully (*geschickt*), clumsily (*ungeschickt*), carefully (*sorgfältig*), etc.

(iv) Try also to use **appropriate adjectives** to describe nouns. This will be particularly valuable if you are able to show that you know the **rules of adjective agreement** summarised below:

1. 'Der' declension
(including DIESER, JEDER, JENER, WELCHER)

	Masculine	Feminine	Neuter	Plural
Nominative	-E	-E	-E	
Accusative		-E	-E	
Genitive				
Dative		**-EN**		

5

2. 'Ein' declension

(including KEIN and possessives MEIN, DEIN, SEIN, IHR, etc.)

	Masculine	Feminine	Neuter	Plural
Nominative	-ER	-E	-ES	
Accusative		-E	-ES	
Genitive			-EN	
Dative				

3. Declension without a preceding article

	Masculine	Feminine	Neuter	Plural
Nominative	-ER	-E	-ES	-E
Accusative	-EN	-E	-ES	-E
Genitive	-EN	-ER	-EN	-ER
Dative	-EM	-ER	-EM	-EN

b) IDIOMS – These can give your composition a feeling of greater naturalness. Idioms grow out of the ways of thinking of speakers of a particular language, and as a result they are often unique to each language: think of "in the soup", "beside oneself" and "to throw in the towel", for which a German will say "in the ink" (*in der Tinte sitzen*), "out of one's little house" (*aus dem Häuschen*) and "to throw one's musket into the corn" (*die Flinte ins Korn werfen*).

Although a word-for-word translation of a German idiom will often sound very odd, this kind of idiom can add to the atmosphere of a composition by its very "German-ness" and by its power to say a great deal in few words. This can highlight particular things felt or observed by a speaker, at moments when maximum effect is called for.

You will find a collection of useful idioms (including those given above) in Section C of the Language Resource Bank at the back of the book.

Part Two
ESSAYS

INTRODUCTORY NOTES

1. Notes on how to write each particular kind of essay are followed by model essays, and then exercises.

2. 150 words was chosen as a useful working number for model essays as this is a typical requirement in Certificate examinations. Your own particular examination may, however, require fewer words. To gain an idea of how a model essay of fewer words would look, reduce or omit portions of the printed model essays as required. If you were required to use a little more than 150 words, only an extra two or three lines would need to be added to the printed model essays.

3. There are altogether 45 essay tasks – 15 picture compositions, 15 stories for continuing and 15 single topic essays.

4. The exercises reflect types which occur regularly in Certificate examinations.

5. The length of the exercises can be varied as required. The suggested lengths are merely guidelines.

6. The exercises could be carried out orally prior to being written.

7. The grammar/vocabulary suggestions are designed to be easily incorporated in the particular essays to which they are attached.

2

Picture Composition

1) THE TASK

Your task is to tell a story suggested by a series of pictures in a range from 60 to about 150 words of accurate and authentic German, and to make your account as interesting to read as possible.

Broadly speaking, the series of pictures that provide the basis for your story suggest situations that are either humorous (practical jokes, comical mishaps, etc.) or unpleasant (danger, rebuke, etc.).

2) CONTENT

a) FREEDOM OF IMAGINATION – The pictures merely serve as an outline for your story. There is no correct interpretation of them as such – you are free to make of them what you wish. Although you may suggest details that are not actually contained in the pictures, the drawings you are given **must** provide the basis and framework for your essay. If you write a story which bears **little relationship** to the pictures, you will be severely penalised on any mark awarded for content.

b) DECIDING ON A STORY – A broad outline of the content can be arrived at by answering the following six questions:

1. WANN? – When does the action take place?
2. WER? – Who are the main characters involved?
3. WO? – Where does the action take place?
4. WAS? – What is it that is of most interest in the story?
5. WARUM? – Why did the situation occur?
6. DANN? – What happens in the end?

c) **MAKING YOUR STORY INTERESTING** – Try to imagine yourself in the situation shown in the pictures, and ask yourself, "How would I feel in that situation? What would I do?" You should try to capture and express moods or reactions (such as surprise, shock, horror, fear, joy or delight) appropriate to the particular situation. A series of bald statements made by an onlooker who feels no real involvement will be lifeless, and will not arouse the interest of the reader. (The **Language Resource Bank** at the back of the book suggests some useful expressions to help you in your choice of the best vocabulary and idioms to use.)

3) STRUCTURE

Having decided in broad outline what the content of your story is going to be, the next step is to consider the way you are going to organise and present your ideas.

a) **A BALANCED ESSAY** – Do not spend too much time writing about the contents of one picture and so leave yourself too few words (bearing in mind the limit allowed) to do justice to the others. If you spend too much time on one at the expense of the others, your essay is likely to be very lopsided.

b) **THE DIVISION OF YOUR ESSAY** – As a general rule, a picture composition can be divided into three roughly equal parts. Each part can consist of one or more paragraphs as appropriate.

i) *Einleitung* – **the introduction**   It has already been suggested that a broad outline for the content of your story could be arrived at by asking yourself six questions. Of these six, the first three – WANN? WER? WO? – would form the introduction to your story.

WANN? – First of all state **when** the story takes place.
The time can be vague:

Eines herrlichen Tages während der Sommerferien . . .
(One magnificent day during the summer holidays . . .)

or more precise:

Letzten Dienstag um drei Uhr nachmittags . . .
(Last Tuesday at three o'clock in the afternoon . . .)

WER?   – When introducing the characters, you can present them in **three possible ways. You could refer to them in general** terms as *Bergsteiger* (climbers), *Wanderer* (hikers), etc. You

9

could explain their relationship to one another, e.g. *Klassen-kameraden* (classmates), *Kusinen* ([girl] cousins), etc. You could also give them names, e.g. *Hans, Inge, Herr Müller, Frau Schmidt,* etc. (You could even, if you wished, make yourself one of the characters, in which case remember to write your essay in the first person – *ich, wir,* etc.)

Where appropriate, give a brief description of the characters, both with regard to their physical appearance and also to the mood they are likely to be in (either because of what they intend to do or because of what they are already doing).

WO?   – Try to give the story as specific a setting as possible.
         For example, instead of merely saying:
         'in den Bergen' (in the mountains)

         say something like:
         'in einem schönen Tal umgeben von hohen Bergen'
         (in a beautiful valley surrounded by high mountains)

ii) *Hauptteil* **– the main part**   In answer to the question WAS? this part will tell us what is of particular interest about the pictures. In answer to the question WARUM? the reason for this interest will be explained.

E.g. WAS?   – *Plötzlich fingen alle Reisenden zu schreien an.*
               (Suddenly all the passengers began to shout.)

WARUM?   – *Der Zug raste durch den Bahnhof, anstatt dort zu halten.*
               (The train sped through the station instead of stopping there.)

As this is the focal point of your essay, it must be as interesting to read as possible. It should especially involve the thoughts, feelings or reactions of the characters, since the situations in which they are involved are usually somewhat out of the ordinary.

iii) *Schluß* **– the conclusion**   If you have aroused the reader's interest and left him wondering how the situation will turn out – DANN? –, make sure that your story does not end in a disappointing anti-climax. Make sure it has a definite conclusion by expressing feelings of satisfaction, relief, gratitude, embarrassment, disappointment, surprise, etc. (whichever is called for by the way events have worked out and the situation of the characters).

B | WRITING A PICTURE COMPOSITION – AN EXAMPLE

Remember that a picture composition can usefully be divided into three

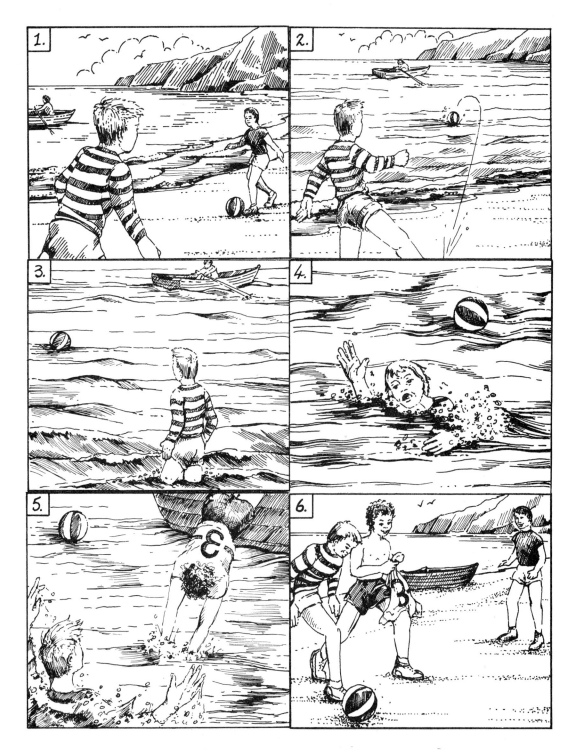

parts. On the following pages is an example of how this can be done for
the series of pictures shown above. Approximately 150 words are
required.

1) EINLEITUNG

Eines herrlichen Tages während der Sommerferien spielten die Brüder Klaus und Gerd Fußball am Travemünder Strand. In einem Ruderboot auf dem Wasser saß ein Junge, der ihrem Spiel interessiert zusah. Plötzlich schoß Klaus den Ball ungeschickt ins Wasser. „Verflixt nochmal!" rief er ärgerlich. „So was Dummes!" [46 words]

ANALYSIS

1. Notice how the introduction answers the questions:

WANN? – *eines herrlichen Tages während der Sommerferien*

WER? – *die Brüder Klaus und Gerd; ein Junge.*

WO? – *am Travemünder Strand; in einem Ruderboot auf der See.*

2. Use of cases
In only 46 words, all the cases have been used:

Nominative: *die Brüder; ein Junge*

Accusative: *den Ball; ins Wasser*

Genitive: *eines . . Tages; während der Sommerferien*

Dative: *am . . Strand; in einem Ruderboot, auf dem Wasser; ihrem Spiel.*

3. Use of verbs
The simple past of one weak verb (*spielen*) and four strong verbs (*sitzen, zusehen, schießen, rufen*) have been used. Of these, notice how *zusehen*, a separable verb, takes the dative.

4. Sentence structure
You can see that in every sentence the word order is different from what we would expect in English. The verbs in the German sentences here all come before their subjects, (e.g. *Plötzlich schoß Klaus*), except in the case of *zusah*, which stands at the end of a relative clause (i.e. a clause beginning with *der, die, das* or their various forms).

5. Use of vocabulary
a) adjectives – *herrlich* with an -en ending shows a good grasp of the rules of adjective agreement.

b) adverbs – To inject interest into a story, words indicating the manner in which something is said or done should be included. In this paragraph, notice the use of *interessiert, plötzlich, ungeschickt* and *ärgerlich*.

c) exclamations – These are useful to express a person's feelings and reactions. In this introduction *"Verflixt nochmal"* and *"So was Dummes"* express Klaus's annoyance with himself.

2) HAUPTTEIL

Ohne lange zu zögern ins Meer lief Klaus. Der ball befand sich aber in tiefem Wasser, und als Klaus auf einmal unterzugehen begann, ergriff ihn eine panische Angst. „Hilfe!" schrie er aus vollem Hals. „Ich kann nicht schwimmen!" Der arme Kerl schwebte wirklich in Lebensgefahr.

[45 words]

ANALYSIS

1. Part Two answers the questions:

WAS? – *. . . als Klaus auf einmal unterzugehen begann, ergriff ihn eine panische Angst.*

WARUM? – *„Ich kann nicht schwimmen!"*

2. Use of cases

Nominative: *der Ball; eine panische Angst; der arme Kerl*

Accusative: *ins Meer; ergriff ihn*

Dative: *in tiefem Wasser; aus vollem Hals*

3. Use of verbs

In addition to strong verbs in the simple past, notice the use of the *ohne . . . zu* construction, and the use of the separable verb *untergehen*. Because *untergehen* is here dependent upon *begann*, it is separated by *zu*.

Notice also the use of the reflexive verb *sich befinden.*

4. Sentence structure

The use of the subordinate clause (beginning: *als Klaus*) preceding a main clause (*ergriff ihn . . .*) demonstrates a mastery of German word order at a very high level (see page 4).

5. Use of vocabulary

a) adjectives – *in tiefem Wasser* demonstrates knowledge of the -em neuter agreement after a dative preposition. Notice how much the use of *panisch* increases the tension in this situation.

b) idioms – the use of *aus vollem Hals* and *schwebte in Lebensgefahr* suggests command of a wide range of vocabulary.

3) SCHLUSS

Der Junge im Ruderboot sah, wie Klaus verzweifelt im Wasser um sich schlug, und er sprang sofort ins Meer, um ihm zu Hilfe zu kommen. In kurzer Zeit gelang es dem Jungen, Klaus ins Boot zu hieven. Die Geschichte nahm ein glückliches Ende – die Brüder hatten einen neuen Freund, mit dem sie fröhlich Fußball spielten! [55 words]

Total: 146 words

ANALYSIS

1. Part three answers the question:
DANN? – *zu Hilfe . . . kommen; ins Boot . . . schleppen; ein glückliches Ende*

2. Use of cases

Nominative: *der Junge; die Geschichte; die Brüder*

Accusative: *um sich; ins Meer; ins Boot; ein glückliches Ende; einen neuen Freund*

Dative: *im Wasser; ihm zu Hilfe; in kurzer Zeit; dem Jungen; mit dem sie . . . spielten.*

3. Use of verbs

Notice the use of the impersonal verb *gelingen* with the dative, and the dative used with the expression *zu Hilfe kommen.*

4. Sentence structure

A number of dependent clauses appear in this concluding section.

i) *. . . sah, wie Klaus . . . schlug*

ii) *. . . um ihm zu Hilfe zu kommen*

iii) *. . . gelang es dem Jungen, Klaus . . . zu hieven*

iv) *. . ., mit dem sie . . . spielten*

5. Use of vocabulary

a) adjectives – *in kurzer Zeit; ein glückliches Ende; einen neuen Freund* show various forms of adjective agreement.

b) *verzweifelt* in the first sentence is balanced by *fröhlich* in the last sentence to show the range of emotions in this section.

4) THE COMPLETE MODEL

Eines herrlichen Tages während der Sommerferien spielten die Brüder Klaus und Gerd Fußball am Travemünder Strand. In einem Ruderboot auf dem Wasser saß ein Junge, der ihrem Spiel interessiert zusah. Plötzlich schoß Klaus den Ball ungeschickt ins Wasser. „Verflixt nochmal!" rief er ärgerlich. „So was Dummes!"

Ohne lange zu zögern, lief Klaus ins Meer. Der Ball befand sich aber in tiefem Wasser, und als Klaus auf einmal unterzugehen begann, ergriff ihn eine panische Angst. „Hilfe!" schrie er aus vollem Hals. „Ich kann nicht schwimmen!" Der arme Kerl schwebte wirklich in Lebensgefahr.

Der Junge im Ruderboot sah, wie Klaus verzweifelt im Wasser um sich schlug, und er sprang sofort ins Meer, um ihm zu Hilfe zu kommen. In kurzer Zeit gelang es dem Jungen, Klaus ins Boot zu hieven. Die Geschichte nahm ein glückliches Ende – die Brüder hatten einen neuen Freund, mit dem sie fröhlich Fußball spielten!

[146 words]

C PICTURE COMPOSITION PRACTICE

In each of the following exercises, write the story depicted by the series of pictures, keeping close to the guideline suggested. (The number of words for each essay may be varied as required.) Suggested vocabulary can be found in the Language Resource Bank under the appropriate headings.

<table>
<tr><td>

1

</td><td>

Write in German, in about 60 words, the story depicted in the series of pictures opposite. State at the end of your essay the number of words used. The story should be in the past tense.

</td></tr>
</table>

Content

Remember:

* Keep your story close to what the pictures show.

* Tell the **whole** story (don't give too much space to one picture).

* Use your imagination – how would **you** feel if it was happening to you?

Structure

Remember:

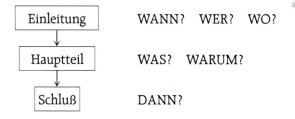

Einleitung	WANN? WER? WO?
Hauptteil	WAS? WARUM?
Schluß	DANN?

Style

In this essay, try particularly to:

* use clauses beginning with *als*, *während* and *weil* (Language Resource Bank, section A.6, "Explanation links").

* use some interesting **Feelings and reactions** vocabulary (L.R.B., section A.2).

* use synonyms for *unglücklich* and *zornig* (L.R.B., section B.1).

2	Write in German, in about 60 words, the story depicted in the series of pictures opposite. State at the end of your essay the number of words used. The story should be in the past tense.

Content

Remember:

* Keep your story close to what the pictures show.

* Tell the **whole** story (don't give too much space to one picture).

* Use your imagination – how would **you** feel if it was happening to you?

Structure

Remember:

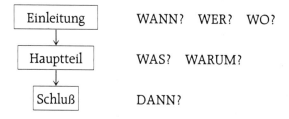

Einleitung	WANN? WER? WO?
Hauptteil	WAS? WARUM?
Schluß	DANN?

Style

In this essay, try particularly to:

* use time links (Language Resource Bank, section A.6).

* use an idiom of **Despair** or **Fear** (L.R.B., sections C.1 and C.4).

* use a synonym for *unglücklich* (L.R.B., section B.1).

19

3	Write in German, in about 60 words, the story depicted in the series of pictures opposite. State at the end of your essay the number of words used. The story should be in the past tense.

Content

Remember:

* Keep your story close to what the pictures show.

* Tell the **whole** story (don't give too much space to one picture).

* Use your imagination – how would **you** feel if it was happening to you?

Structure

Remember:

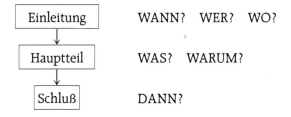

Einleitung   WANN?   WER?   WO?

Hauptteil   WAS?   WARUM?

Schluß   DANN?

Style

In this essay, try particularly to:

* follow the Time–Manner–Place (WANN?–WIE?–WO?) rule (see Chapter One, section B.2, p.5).

* use two verbs of **Activity, behaviour** (Language Resource Bank, section A.4).

* use time links (L.R.B., section A.6).

YREB, June 1981

<table>
<tr><td>**4**</td><td>Write in German, in about 80 words, the story depicted in the series of pictures opposite. State at the end of your essay the number of words used. The story should be in the past tense.</td></tr>
</table>

Content

Remember:

* Keep your story close to what the pictures show.

* Tell the **whole** story (don't give too much space to one picture).

* Use your imagination – how would **you** feel if it was happening to you?

Structure

Remember:

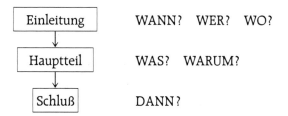

Einleitung	WANN? WER? WO?
Hauptteil	WAS? WARUM?
Schluß	DANN?

Style

In this essay, try particularly to:

* use some interesting **Feelings and reactions** vocabulary (Language Resource Bank, section A.2).

* use an exclamation (L.R.B., section A.3).

* use clauses beginning with *nachdem* and *weil* (L.R.B., section A.6. "Explanation links").

<table>
<tr><td>**5**</td><td>Write in German, in about 100 words, the story depicted in the series of pictures opposite. State at the end of your essay the number of words used. The story should be in the past tense.</td></tr>
</table>

Content

Remember:

* Keep your story close to what the pictures show.

* Tell the **whole** story (don't give too much space to one picture).

* Use your imagination – how would **you** feel if it was happening to you?

Structure

Remember:

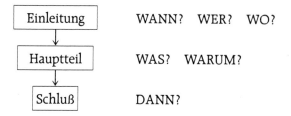

Einleitung	WANN? WER? WO?
Hauptteil	WAS? WARUM?
Schluß	DANN?

Style

In this essay, try particularly to:

* use time links (Language Resource Bank, section A.6).

* use synonyms for *glücklich* and *unglücklich* (L.R.B., section B.1).

* use an expression from the **Schluß** section (L.R.B., A.5).

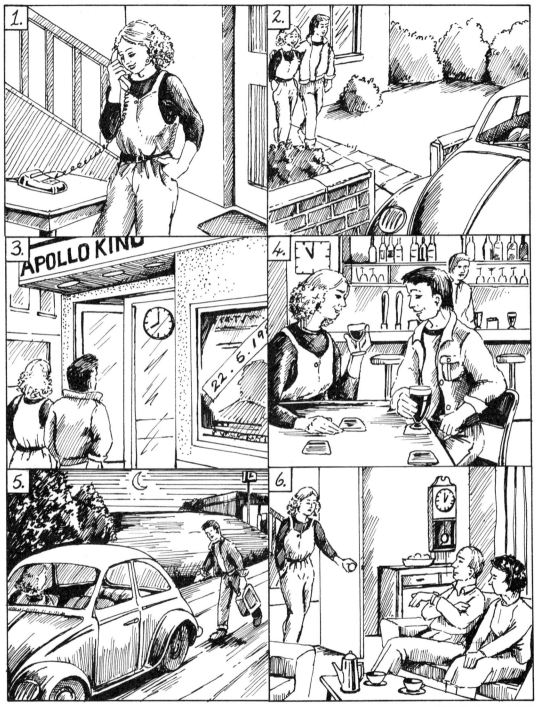

SWEB, May 1982

6	Write in German, in about 150 words, the story depicted in the series of pictures opposite. State at the end of your essay the number of words used. The story should be in the past tense.

Content

Remember:

* Keep your story close to what the pictures show.

* Tell the **whole** story (don't give too much space to one picture).

* Use your imagination – how would **you** feel if it was happening to you?

Structure

Remember:

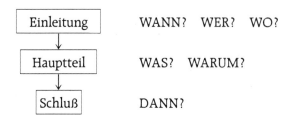

Style

In this essay, try particularly to:

* use clauses beginning with *als* and *während* (Language Resource Bank, section A.6, "Explanation links").

* use an exclamation (L.R.B., section A.3).

* use some interesting **Feelings and reactions** vocabulary (L.R.B., Section A.2).

<table>
<tr><td>

7

</td><td>

Write in German, in about 150 words, the story depicted in the series of pictures opposite. State at the end of your essay the number of words used. The story should be in the past tense.

</td></tr>
</table>

Content

Remember:

* Keep your story close to what the pictures show.

* Tell the **whole** story (don't give too much space to one picture).

* Use your imagination – how would **you** feel if it was happening to you?

Structure

Remember:

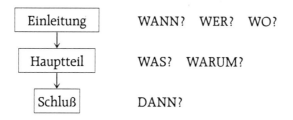

Einleitung	WANN? WER? WO?
Hauptteil	WAS? WARUM?
Schluß	DANN?

Style

In this essay, try particularly to:

* use the particles *nur* and *wohl* (Language Resource Bank, section B.2).

* use two verbs of **Activity, behaviour** (L.R.B., section A.4).

* use synonyms for *sagen* and *zornig* (L.R.B., section B.1).

8	Write in German, in about 150 words, the story depicted in the series of pictures opposite. State at the end of your essay the number of words used. The story should be in the past tense.

Content

Remember:

* Keep your story close to what the pictures show.

* Tell the **whole** story (don't give too much space to one picture).

* Use your imagination – how would **you** feel if it was happening to you?

Structure

Remember:

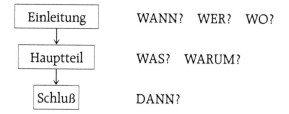

Einleitung	WANN? WER? WO?
Hauptteil	WAS? WARUM?
Schluß	DANN?

Style

In this essay, try particularly to:

* use time links (Language Resource Bank, section A.6).

* use some interesting **Feelings and reactions** vocabulary (L.R.B., section A.2).

* use an idiom of **Surprise** (L.R.B., section C.8).

9	Write in German, in about 150 words, the story depicted in the series of pictures opposite. State at the end of your essay the number of words used. The story should be in the past tense.

Content

Remember:

* Keep your story close to what the pictures show.

* Tell the **whole** story (don't give too much space to one picture).

* Use your imagination – how would **you** feel if it was happening to you?

Structure

Remember:

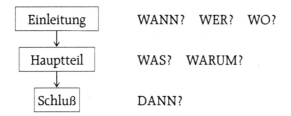

Einleitung	WANN? WER? WO?
Hauptteil	WAS? WARUM?
Schluß	DANN?

Style

In this essay, try particularly to:

* use an idiom of **Happiness, pleasure** (Language Resource Bank, section C.5).

* use clauses beginning with *als, nachdem* and *während* (L.R.B., section A.6, "Explanation links").

* use two verbs of **Activity, behaviour** (L.R.B., section A.4).

	Write in German, in about 150 words, the story depicted in the series of pictures opposite. State at the end of your essay the number of words used. The story should be in the past tense.
10	

Content

Remember:

* Keep your story close to what the pictures show.

* Tell the **whole** story (don't give too much space to one picture).

* Use your imagination – how would **you** feel if it was happening to you?

Structure

Remember:

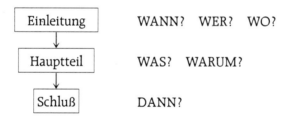

Einleitung   WANN? WER? WO?

Hauptteil   WAS? WARUM?

Schluß   DANN?

Style

In this essay, try particularly to:

* use a synonym for *schlecht* and an idiom of **Humour, ridicule** (Language Resource Bank, sections B.1 and C.6).

* use two verbs of **Acitivity, behaviour** (L.R.B., section A.4).

* use clauses beginning with *als, da* and *um . . . zu* (L.R.B., section A.,6, "Explanation links").

Ein unartiges Kind

WJEC, June 1981

<table>
<tr><td>

11
</td><td>
Write in German, in about 150 words, the story depicted in the series of pictures opposite. State at the end of your essay the number of words used. The story should be in the past tense.
</td></tr>
</table>

Content

Remember:

* ✱ Keep your story close to what the pictures show.
* ✱ Tell the **whole** story (don't give too much space to one picture).
* ✱ Use your imagination – how would **you** feel if it was happening to you?

Structure

Remember:

Einleitung	WANN? WER? WO?
↓	
Hauptteil	WAS? WARUM?
↓	
Schluß	DANN?

Style

In this essay, try particularly to:

* ✱ use clauses beginning with *als* and *nachdem* (Language Resource Bank, section A.6., "Explanation links").
* ✱ use an exclamation (L.R.B., section A.3).'
* ✱ use an idiom of **Surprise** (L.R.B., section C.8).

12	Write in German, in about 150 words, the story depicted in the series of pictures opposite. State at the end of your essay the number of words used. The story should be in the past tense.

Content

Remember:

* Keep your story close to what the pictures show.

* Tell the **whole** story (don't give too much space to one picture).

* Use your imagination – how would **you** feel if it was happening to you?

Structure

Remember:

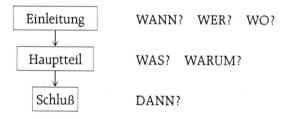

Einleitung — WANN?   WER?   WO?

Hauptteil — WAS?   WARUM?

Schluß — DANN?

Style

In this essay, try particularly to:

* use interesting **Feelings and reactions** vocabulary (Language Resource Bank, section A.2).

* use synonyms for *glücklich, schlecht* and *gut* (L.R.B., section B.1).

* use the particles *etwa* and *wohl* (L.R.B., section B2).

38

SWEB, May 1983

13	Write in German, in about 150 words, the story depicted in the series of pictures opposite. State at the end of your essay the number of words used. The story should be in the past tense.

Content

Remember:

* Keep your story close to what the pictures show.

* Tell the **whole** story (don't give too much space to one picture).

* Use your imagination – how would **you** feel if it was happening to you?

Structure

Remember:

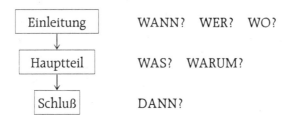

Einleitung	WANN? WER? WO?
Hauptteil	WAS? WARUM?
Schluß	DANN?

Style

In this essay, try particularly to:

* use an idiom of **Happiness, pleasure** (Language Resource Bank, section C.5).

* use some interesting **Activity, behaviour** vocabulary (L.R.B., section A.4).

* use the future tense.

Bei der Arbeit denkt man an die Diskothek

O&C, July 1981

<table>
<tr><td>

14

</td><td>

Write in German, in about 150 words, the story depicted in the series of pictures opposite. State at the end of your essay the number of words used. The story should be in the past tense.

</td></tr>
</table>

Content

Remember:

* Keep your story close to what the pictures show.

* Tell the **whole** story (don't give too much space to one picture).

* Use your imagination – how would **you** feel if it was happening to you?

Structure

Remember:

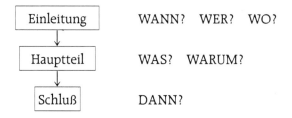

Einleitung	WANN? WER? WO?
Hauptteil	WAS? WARUM?
Schluß	DANN?

Style

In this essay, try particularly to:

* use synonyms for *sagen, gut, unglücklich* (Language Resource Bank, section B.1).

* use clauses introduced by *um . . . zu* and *während* (L.R.B., section A.6., "Explanation links").

* use an exclamation (L.R.B., section A.3).

	Write in German, in about 150 words, the story depicted in the series of pictures opposite. State at the end of your essay the number of words used. The story should be in the past tense.
15	

Content

Remember:

* Keep your story close to what the pictures show.

* Tell the **whole** story (don't give too much space to one picture).

* Use your imagination – how would **you** feel if it was happening to you?

Structure

Remember:

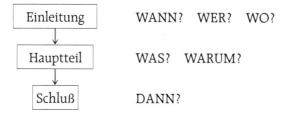

Einleitung	WANN? WER? WO?
Hauptteil	WAS? WARUM?
Schluß	DANN?

Style

In this essay, try particularly to:

* use the pluperfect tense.

* use an exclamation (Language Resource Bank, section A.3).

* use an expression from the **Schluß** section (L.R.B., section A.5).

Selbst erfolglose Angler müssen etwas nach Hause mitbringen

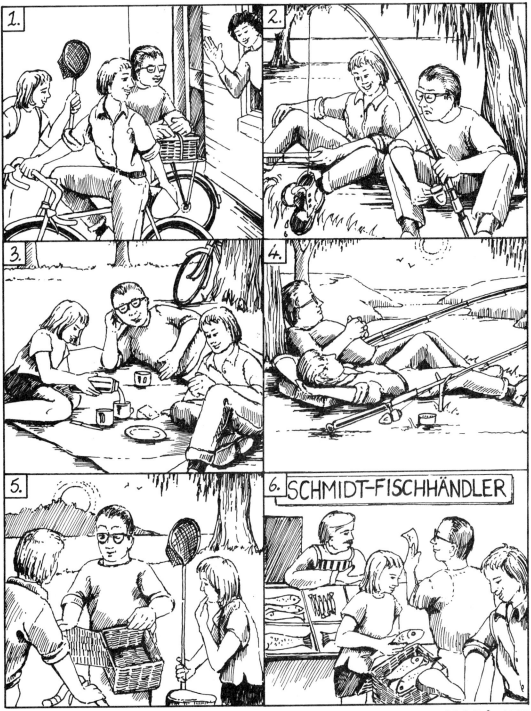

O&C, July 1982

3

Continuing a Story

A | APPROACHES

1) THE TASK

You are given an introductory sentence or paragraph in German which you are told to continue in the form of a story. You are allowed a limited number of words, usually somewhere between 100 and 150.

Usually the kind of story you are required to write involves something out of the ordinary. Indeed, the opening sentence of an introductory paragraph in one past examination paper actually began: 'Etwas Seltsames geschah letztes Jahr . . .'. The kind of story that is set may deal with a dangerous or threatening situation, an unexpected discovery, a criminal or suspicious activity, a pleasant or unpleasant surprise, etc.

2) CONTENT

a) FREEDOM OF IMAGINATION – This kind of writing task allows you much greater freedom of imagination than does a picture composition, which gives you a fixed framework for your story. From the opening line or paragraph you are given, you can develop your story in any way you choose. Before you begin to write, however, make sure you know how your story will end. If you know you are short of the vocabulary you need for the story that you would like to write, **choose another story line that will best show off your knowledge of German**. Remember: although imagination will play a far greater rôle in this kind of composition than in a picture composition, it is still your command of German that the examiner is most interested in.

b) DECIDING ON A STORY – First of all, and most important: make sure that you **continue** what you have been given as an introduction.

Beware of making the common mistake of turning part of the introduction into a story on its own. For example, if you are told:

> *Als Kurt eines Tages unterwegs in die Stadt war, um eine neue Angelrute zu kaufen, bemerkte er plötzlich, daß ein Mann mit einer Pistole vor einer Bank stand . . .*

do **not** write about Kurt's interest in fishing! Also, do not include the introduction in your story. Proceed **from** it.

When deciding on a continuation for a story, it might be useful to ask yourself the following questions:

    1. WIE? – How does the person react to the situation?
    2. WAS? – What does he or she do?
    3. WARUM? – Why does he or she do this?
    4. DANN? – What happens in the end?

c) **MAKING YOUR STORY INTERESTING** – Because your story does not have to be factually true, you can create situations that will really highlight a character's feelings and reactions. This kind of composition encourages you to use adjectives and verbs conveying shock, horror, dismay, or joy and delight. As with picture compositions, you must imagine your characters' feelings if your story is not to be flat or lifeless. This should be easier than in picture compositions, because **you** create the situation your characters are in. (The Language Resource Bank at the back of the book suggests some useful expressions to help you in your choice of the best vocabulary and idioms to use.)

3) STRUCTURE

a) **A BALANCED ESSAY** – Make sure that you do not dwell too long on one aspect of your story. For instance, do not spend so much time describing a character's feelings or state of mind that you are left with too little space to tell what actually **happens** in the story.

b) **THE DIVISION OF YOUR ESSAY** – You can usefully divide the content of your story into three parts. Each part can consist of one or more paragraphs as appropriate.

i) *Einleitung* — **the introduction** In this you can finish setting the scene by adding further details to those already given. e.g.

> *Als Kurt eines Tages unterwegs in die Stadt war, um eine neue Angelrute zu kaufen, bemerkte er, daß ein Mann mit einer Pistole vor einer Bank stand . . . Erzählen Sie weiter.*

You could continue this by adding information about the man – his appearance, his expression (nervous, tense, etc.); his manner (cautious, suspicious, etc.); about the street – deserted because of the afternoon heat, etc., quiet because it was off the main road or because it was lunchtime, etc; about the bank – its position, its size, etc.

In answer to the question WIE? you could then describe Kurt's feelings and reactions to the situation, i.e. the thoughts that ran through his mind, the action he proposed to take, etc.

ii) *Hauptteil* — **the main part**   This will answer the questions WAS? – what course of action was taken and WARUM? – why this action was taken. You could proceed with the story of Kurt, for instance, by making him into a hero. He could surprise and disarm the man himself because there was no phone box at hand from which to inform the police. Or you could take a more conventional line by getting him to phone the police because he did not think it wise to take any personal action.

iii) *Schluß* — **the conclusion**   This will answer the question DANN?, telling us of the final outcome of events. Kurt, for instance, could be put forward as a hero, making newspaper headlines, or he could be given a reward by the bank for his prompt action in phoning the police. Whatever ending you choose, make sure that it is consistent with the beginning of the story and does not drift so far away from your starting point that it no longer fits the story.

Make sure, too, that it does not end in a disappointing anti-climax. Describe feelings of satisfaction, relief, gratitude, etc. (whichever is called for by the ending you have given the story and the characters' parts in it) so that it ends on a definite note.

B   CONTINUING A STORY – AN EXAMPLE

Remember that an essay of this type can usefully be divided into three parts. Below is an example of how this can be done for an essay of about 150 words.

QUESTION   –   *Als Kurt eines Tages unterwegs in die Stadt war, um eine neue Angelrute zu kaufen, bemerkte er plötzlich, daß ein Mann mit einer Pistole vor einer Bank stand . . .*

Continue the story in German in about 150 words.

1) EINLEITUNG

Die Straßen waren fast leer, weil es so fürchterlich heiß war. Der Mann hatte wahrscheinlich geglaubt, daß ihn niemand stören würde. Nervös sah er sich um, dann ging er langsam und vorsichtig in die Bank.

Kurt zitterte vor Aufregung. Nirgends war eine Telefonzelle zu sehen. Was sollte er nur machen? [50 words]

ANALYSIS

Notice how the introduction tells us more about the man, and also, in answer to the question WIE?, something about Kurt's feelings and appraisal of the situation.

1. Use of cases
Notice the use of the accusative object pronoun *ihn*, the accusative reflexive pronoun *sich*, and the accusative of motion after the preposition *in*.

2. Use of verbs
Notice the variety of tenses: imperfect of *sein, gehen, zittern*, and the reflexive verb *sich umsehen*; the pluperfect of *glauben*; the conditional of *stören*; the passive use of the infinitive *sehen*; and the subjunctive of *können*.

3. Sentence structure
Two subordinate clauses have been used, one introduced by *weil* the other by *daß*. Twice there has been an inversion of subject and verb – *Nervös sah er sich um*, and *dann ging er*.

4. Use of vocabulary
Notice how an intensity of feeling is developed by the use of such words and expressions as *fürchterlich heiß – nervös – langsam und vorsichtig – zitterte vor Aufregung – Was könnte er nur machen?*

Ohne lange zu zögern, entschloß sich Kurt, sich hinter einem Auto zu verstecken, das direkt vor dem Bankeingang geparkt war. „Vielleicht kann ich ihn überraschen, wenn er aus der Bank kommt", dachte er sich. „Er hat ja keine Ahnung, daß ihn jemand gesehen hat, und er wird auf den Angriff nicht gefaßt sein." [53 words]

ANALYSIS

This part answers the questions:

WAS? – *entschloß sich Kurt, sich hinter einem Auto zu verstecken*

WARUM? – *„vielleicht kann ich ihn überrashen"*

1. Use of cases

Accusative: *ihn überraschen; keine Ahnung; ihn gesehen; den Angriff*

Dative: *hinter einem Auto; vor dem Bankeingang; aus der Bank; dachte er sich*

2. Use of verbs

Notice the use of *zu* after *ohne*, and *zu* before the infinitive in clauses following such verbs as *hoffen, entschließen* etc.

Notice, too, the variety in tenses:

present – *kann, kommt, hat*
imperfect – *entschloß, war, dachte*
perfect – *. . . gesehen hat*
future – *er wird . . . erwarten*

There are also two kinds of reflexive verbs: with the accusative reflexive pronoun: *sich verstecken*; and with the dative reflexive form: *sich denken*.

3. Sentence structure

There are a number of dependent clauses revealing a mastery of the rules of word order. There is the infinitive clause after *entschloß sich Kurt*; the relative clause *hinter einem Auto . . ., das*; and two subordinate clauses, one after *wenn*, the other after *da*. In addition there are three instances of inversion of subject and verb (verb coming before its subject).

4. Use of vocabulary

The linking expression *ohne lange zu zögern* shows the relationship between parts 1 and 2.

Notice the development of the idea of surprising someone – *sich verstecken; . . . ihn überraschen; . . . keine Ahnung; nicht gefaßt*.

The use of the particle *ja* adds a touch of "Germanness" to the final sentence.

3) SCHLUSS

Mit klopfendem Herzen wartete Kurt auf den richtigen Augenblick. Als er den Bankräuber rückwärts aus der Bank kommen sah, sprang er blitzschnell hinter dem Auto hervor und schlug ihm die Pistole aus der Hand. Erschrocken ließ der Räuber die Geldsäcke fallen und lief davon.

Am nächsten Tag erschien die Geschichte vom tapferen Kurt in allen Tageszeitungen! [56 words]

ANALYSIS

This part answers the question DANN?, telling us what happens in the end.

1. Use of cases
Nominative: *der Räuber; die Geschichte*
Accusative: *den . . . Augenblick; den Bankräuber, die Pistole; die Geldsäcke*
Dative: *mit klopfendem Herzen; hinter dem Auto; aus der Hand; am nächsten Tag; vom tapferen Kurt; in allen Tageszeitungen*

2. Use of verbs
Although all the verbs are in the imperfect tense, they show considerable variety. Thus, we find three separable verbs – *abwarten, davonlaufen, hervorspringen;* the double verb *fallenlassen;* and *schlagen* plus the dative.

3. Sentence structure
There is an example of a subordinate clause introducing a main clause (*Als er ... sah, sprang er ...*), and there are three instances of inversion of subject and verb.

4. Use of vocabulary
Mastery of the rules of adjective agreement is shown by the following:
mit klopfendem Herzen
auf den richtigen Augenblick
am nächsten Tag
vom tapferen Kurt
in allen Tageszeitungen

Notice how the adjectives, adverbs, and verbs chosen help to create atmosphere by suggesting emotional states and rapidity of action. *Mit klopfendem Herzen, sprang . . . blitzschnell . . . hervor, schlug, erschrocken, ließ . . . fallen, lief davon* and *die Geschichte vom tapferen Kurt* all add to the mood and pace of the story.

4) THE COMPLETE MODEL

QUESTION – *Als Kurt eines Tages unterwegs in die Stadt war, um eine neue Angelrute zu kaufen, bemerkte er plötzlich, daß ein Mann mit einer Pistole vor einer Bank stand . . .* Continue the story in German in about 150 words.

CONTINUATION – *Die Straßen waren fast leer, weil es so fürchterlich heiß war. Der Mann hatte wahrscheinlich geglaubt, daß ihn niemand stören würde. Nervös sah er sich um, dann ging er langsam und vorsichtig in die Bank.*

Kurt zitterte vor Aufregung. Nirgends war eine Telefonzelle zu sehen. Was sollte er nur machen?

Ohne lange zu zögern, entschloß sich Kurt, sich hinter einem Auto zu verstecken, das direkt vor der Bank geparkt war. „Vielleicht kann ich ihn überraschen, wenn er aus der Bank kommt", dachte er sich. „Er hat ja keine Ahnung, daß ihn jemand gesehen hat, und er wird auf den Angriff nicht gefaßt sein."

Mit klopfendem Herzen wartete Kurt auf den richtigen Augenblick. Als er den Bankräuber rückwarts aus der Bank kommen sah, sprang er blitzschnell hinter dem Auto hervor und schlug ihm die Pistole aus der Hand. Erschrocken ließ der Räuber die Geldsäcke fallen und lief davon.

Am nächsten Tag erschien die Geschichte vom tapferen Kurt in allen Tages-zeitungen!   [159 words]

In all the questions below, continue the story in German using about 150 words (more, or less, if required). Suggested vocabulary can be found in the Language Resource Bank at the back of the book.

Content

Remember:

* Continue from the introduction you are given (don't go off on a different tack).

* Make sure you know how your story will end before you start.

* Make sure you have the vocabulary to tell the story you have decided on.

* Tell a balanced story – describe the characters' feelings, but leave yourself enough words to tell the story as well!

* Use your imagination – how would you feel if it happened to you?

Structure

Remember:

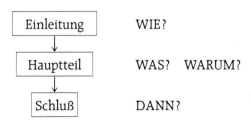

Einleitung	WIE?
Hauptteil	WAS? WARUM?
Schluß	DANN?

1	*Als Johann erfuhr, daß er sitzenbleiben würde, stand er wie vom Donner gerührt da. „Was werde ich meinen Eltern sagen?" dachte er sich. . . .*

In this essay, try particularly to:

✻ use explanation links (Language Resource Bank, section A.6).

✻ use idioms of **Disapproval, displeasure** and **Rebukes** (L.R.B., sections C.3 and C.7).

✻ use the particles *eben, mal* and *so* (L.R.B., section B.2).

2	*Manfred lief Hals über Kopf zum Bahnhof, um seinen Zug noch zu erreichen. Er hatte vergessen, daß heute das Sportfest stattfand. . . .*

In this essay, try particularly to:

✻ use exclamations (Language Resource Bank, section A.3).

✻ use synonyms for *unglücklich* and *sagen* (L.R.B., section B.1).

✻ use an expression from the **Schluß** section (L.R.B., section A.5).

3	*Birgit setzte sich auf ihren Eckplatz im Zug und freute sich über die Reise nach Paris. Plötzlich erinnerte sie sich, daß sie ihren Reisepaß vergessen hatte! . . .*

In this essay, try particularly to:

✻ use exclamations (Language Resource Bank, section A.3).

✻ use idioms of **Humour, ridicule** and **Rebukes** (L.R.B., sections C.6 and C.7).

✻ use explanation links (L.R.B., section A.6).

4	*Anna war furchtbar enttäuscht, daß ihr Freund Helmut anscheinend ihren Geburtstag vergessen hatte. Das Telefon klingelte. Ihre Mutter nahm den Hörer ab, dann sagte sie Anna: „Helmut am Apparat. Er will dich sprechen."* . . .

In this essay, try particularly to:

* use some interesting **Feelings and reactions** vocabulary (Language Resource Bank, section A.2).

* use synonyms for *gut/schlecht, glücklich/unglücklich* (L.R.B., section B.1).

* use the particles *doch, eben* and *schon* (L.R.B., section B.2).

5	*Norbert öffnete den Brief und begann zu lesen. Einige Sekunden später rief er erfreut: „Onkel Heinrich kommt morgen aus der Schweiz. Er ist auf Geschäftsreise und bleibt ein paar Tage in Hamburg!"* . . .

In this essay, try particulary to:

* use some interesting **Feelings and reactions** vocabulary (Language Resource Bank, section A.2).

* use time links (L.R.B., section A.6).

* use the particles *etwa, schon* and *so* (L.R.B., section B.2).

6	*Die Reise war schrecklich, und Hans hatte Kopfschmerzen. Er wollte nur schlafen gehen, aber als er im Dorf ankam, erfuhr er, daß alle Hotels völlig ausgebucht waren.* . . . .

In this essay, try particularly to:

* use some interesting **Feelings and reactions** vocabulary (Language Resource Bank, section A.2).

* use time links (L.R.B., section A.6).

* use an expression from the **Schluß** section (L.R.B., section A.5).

<table>
<tr><td>**7**</td><td>*Fritz und Udo machten eine Radtour auf dem Land. Plötzlich hatte Udos Fahrrad eine Reifenpanne. Dummerweise hatten die zwei Jungen kein Flickzeug mitgebracht. Bis zum nächsten Ort waren es noch mehr als zwanzig Kilometer. . . .*</td></tr>
</table>

In this essay, try particularly to:

* use synonyms for *unglücklich* and *zornig* (Language Resource Bank, section B.1).

* use the particles *doch, eben* and *ja* (L.R.B., section B.2).

* use an expression from the **Schluß** section (L.R.B., section A.5).

<table>
<tr><td>**8**</td><td>*Auf der Rückfahrt vom Schiurlaub mußte die Schulgruppe in Zürich umsteigen. In fünf Minuten sollte der letzte Zug abfahren, aber ein Schüler fehlte noch. Der Lehrer sah besorgt auf die Uhr. . .*</td></tr>
</table>

In this essay, try particularly to:

* use some interesting **Activity, behaviour** vocabulary (Language Resource Bank, section A.4).

* use time links (L.R.B., section A.6).

* use synonyms for *zornig, sagen* and *unglücklich* (L.R.B., section B.1).

<table>
<tr><td>**9**</td><td>*Karen hätte sich monatelang auf den Besuch zu ihrer Austausch-partnerin gefreut, denn sie war noch nie in Deutschland gewesen. Endlich kam der Tag der Abfahrt. . . .*</td></tr>
</table>

In this essay, try particularly to:

* use some interesting **Feelings and reactions** vocabulary (Language Resource Bank, section A.2).

* use synonyms for *gut* and *glücklich* (L.R.B., section B.1).

* use appropriate time links (L.R.B., section A.6).

10 *Heute sollten die Freunde Richard und Helmut bergsteigen gehen, aber als sie zum Fenster hinaussahen, bemerkten sie, daß in der Nacht zwei oder drei Zentimeter Schnee gefallen waren. Trotzdem entschieden sie sich, nach dem Frühstück in der Jugendherberge in die Berge zu gehen. . . .*

In this essay, try particularly to:

* use some appropriate **Activity, behaviour** vocabulary (Language Resource Bank, section A.4).

* use idioms of **Despair** and **Difficulties, danger** (L.R.B., sections C.1 and C.2).

* use the particles *etwa, ja* and *schon* (L.R.B., section B.2).

11 *Es war Walters erster Schultag. Als seine Mutter sagte: „Komm Walter, wir gehen jetzt zur Schule", fing er zu weinen an. . . .*

In this essay, try particularly to:

* use interesting **Feelings and reactions** vocabulary (Language Resource Bank, section A.2).

* use interesting **Activity, behaviour** vocabulary (L.R.B., section A.4).

* use clauses introduced by *nachdem* and *als* (L.R.B., section A.6).

12 *Peter war noch nie mit einer Seilbahn gefahren, und jetzt im Urlaub in der Schweiz hatte er die Gelegenheit, mit Freunden zum Schilthorngipfel hinaufzufahren. Leider aber hatte er eine furchtbare Höhenangst, und als er auf die Seilbahn wartete, begann er unkontrollierbar zu zittern. . . .*

In this essay, try particularly to:

* use explanation links (Language Resource Bank, section A.6).

* use the particles *doch, nur* and *schon* (L.R.B., section B.2).

* use idioms of **Fear** and **Humour, ridicule** (L.R.B., sections C.4 and C.6).

| 13 | *Der Zug fuhr planmäßig in den Hamburger Hauptbahnhof ein. David stieg aus und sah sich nach seinem Brieffreund um, der ihn abholen sollte. Er war nicht zu sehen. Zwanzig Minuten später war noch immer neimand da. David war zum ersten Mal in Hamburg. . . .* |

In this essay, try particularly to:

*   use interesting **Activity, behaviour** vocabulary (Language Resource Bank, section A.4).

*   use explanation links (L.R.B., section A.6).

*   use an expression from the **Schluß** section (L.R.B., section A.5).

| 14 | *Es war spät am Abend, und Maria war allein im Haus. Plötzlich sah sie eine dunkle Gestalt am Fenster. . . .* |

In this essay, try particularly to:

*   use some interesting **Feelings and reactions** vocabulary (Language Resource Bank, section A.2).

*   use some time links (L.R.B., section A.6).

*   use idioms of **Despair** and **Fear** (L.R.B., sections C.1 and C.4).

| 15 | *Auf einem Spaziergang mit seinem Hund sah Gerd einen verdächtigen Mann im Wald, der einen Haufen Papiere verbrannte. Gerd versteckte sich hinter einem Baum und wartete, bis der Mann fortging. Als Gerd die verbrannten Papiere überprüfte, bemerkte er, daß ein Blatt noch lesbar war. Oben standen die Wörter „STRENG GEHEIM". Plötzlich begann sein Hund zu bellen. . . .* |

In this essay, try particularly to:

*   use some interesting **Feelings and reactions** vocabulary (Language Resource Bank, section A.2).

*   use some interesting **Activity, behaviour** vocabulary (L.R.B., section A.4).

*   use time links (L.R.B., section A.6).

4

Single-topic Essays

1) THE TASK

You are asked to write on a given subject, which will usually be based on a situation taken from your personal experience. This can include such things as moving house; a visit to the theatre; a camping holiday; a book you have recently read; a typical school day; etc. The number of words allowed for this task is usually between 50 and 150.

2) CONTENT

a) FREEDOM OF IMAGINATION – Your account does not necessarily have to be based entirely on your personal experience. Although you will probably want to write about things that you know about from experience, you may include imaginary details and events if you wish. Remember: while the quality of your imagination will help make your essay interesting, what matters most is the kind of German that you write. Only write about the things you can handle with your grasp of German vocabulary and grammar.

b) DECIDING ON THE CONTENT – It would be a good idea to jot down, more or less in order, the key words or phrases that will form the basis of your essay. For instance, if you were asked to write about a school skiing trip to Austria, you could produce a skeleton such as this:

Osterferien — zehn Tage — Schulgruppe — Alpen — Berggasthof — Reise — Wetter — Schi fahren — Spaß — lustig — Abreise — schweren Herzens

59

The examination paper will sometimes give you a skeleton such as this to help you get started, but more usually you will have to make one up for yourself. You can do this by asking yourself the following questions:

1. **WANN?** – When did the events take place?
2. **WER?** – Who were the people involved?
3. **WO?** – Where did the events take place?
4. **WAS?** – What were the most important things that happened?
5. **WIE?** – How did the people involved react to these things?
6. **DANN?** – How did everything end?

c) **MAKING YOUR STORY INTERESTING** – Try to avoid the "shopping list" approach. It is tempting when writing an essay such as this to report events one after the other as they occur to you.

Your approach should be much more that of a diary, in which you record your feelings and reactions to events as well as the events themselves. When writing your essay, try to re-live the incidents and moments that you are recording, and attempt to share your feelings of happiness, pleasure, surprise, disappointment, etc. with the reader. If you are working from your imagination rather than your memory, try to put across how you think you might have felt and reacted in the circumstances you describe. (The Language Resource Bank at the back of the book suggests some useful expressions to help you in your choice of the best vocabulary and idioms to use.)

3) STRUCTURE

a) **A BALANCED ESSAY** – Do not spend too much time talking about one aspect of your account at the expense of other equally important ones. For instance, if writing about a school trip, don't spend too long describing the journey and then find yourself with too few words left to do justice to describing your activities. Also, avoid the temptation to repeat yourself, e.g. by saying much the same thing about the homeward journey as you did about the outward journey.

b) **THE DIVISION OF YOUR ESSAY** – You can usefully divide the content of your essay into three more or less equal parts. Each part can consist of one or more paragraphs, as appropriate.

60

i) *Einleitung* – **the introduction** To set the scene in topic essays you can ask yourself the first three of the questions suggested above – WANN? WER? WO? In an essay about a school ski trip, this would give you such key words as:

WANN? – *Osterferien; zehn Tage*
WER? – *Schulgruppe*
WO? – *Alpen; Berggasthof*

ii) *Hauptteil* – **the main part** This will answer the questions WAS? – what were the most important things that happened during the period in question, and WIE? – how did the people involved react to these things?

If you were writing the essay about the school ski trip, your skeleton could be continued as follows:

WAS? – *Reise – Wetter – Schi fahren*
WIE? – *Spaß – lustig*

iii) *Schluß* – **the conclusion** This will tell us about how things came to an end, in answer to the question DANN? In any essay involving a trip or visit, the most likely ending will have something to do with the journey home.

In almost all kinds of single-topic essays, you can conclude by saying something about the way the particular people felt after the experience they had just had.

B | WRITING A SINGLE-TOPIC ESSAY – AN EXAMPLE

QUESTION – Write in German an essay of about 150 words describing a school ski trip to Austria or Switzerland.

PLAN – *Osterferien — zehn Tage — Schulgruppe — Alpen — Berggasthof — Reise — Wetter — Schi fahren — Spaß — lustig — Abreise — schweren Herzens*

1) EINLEITUNG

Unser Deutschlehrer organisierte jedes Jahr in den Osterferien einen zehntägigen Schiurlaub in Österreich. Dieses Jahr war ich einer der Glücklichen, die einen Platz bekamen. Unsere Schulgruppe bestand aus dreißig Teilnehmern, die sich monatelang mit großer Begeisterung auf den Aufenthalt in einem reizenden Berggasthof hoch in den Alpen gefreut hatten.

[49 words]

ANALYSIS

This part answers the questions WANN? WER? WO?

1. Use of cases

Nominative: *unser Deutschlehrer; jedes Jahr; einer; unsere Schulgruppe*

Accusative: *dieses Jahr; einen zehntägigen Schiurlaub; einen Platz; den Aufenthalt*

Genitive: *. . . der Glücklichen*

Dative: *in den Osterferien; aus dreißig Teilnehmern; mit großer Begeisterung; in einem reizenden Berggasthof; in den Alpen*

2. Use of verbs

Although the imperfect is mostly used throughout, the verbs themselves are quite varied in that we find a weak verb (*organisieren*), two strong verbs (*bekommen, bestehen*) and a reflexive verb with a preposition (*sich freuen auf*) used in the pluperfect tense.

3. Sentence structure

Notice the use of the relative clauses beginning with *der* and *die*.

The last sentence in particular reveals a mastery of the rules of word order in that we see:

i) correct position of the verb *freuten* at the end of the relative clause introduced by *die*.

ii) the Time–Manner–Place (WANN?–WIE?–WO?) rule observed: *monatelang – mit großer Begeisterung – den Aufenthalt in einem reizenden Berggasthof.*

In the second sentence we find an example of inversion of subject and verb: *Dieses Jahr war ich . . .*

4. Use of vocabulary

It is not enough simply to list bare facts. Notice how the choice of vocabulary creates a distinct atmosphere of pleasure and expectation:

einer der Glücklichen; mit großer Begeisterung; sich freuen auf; in einem reizenden Berggasthof.

Mastery of the rules of adjective agreement is shown in several instances:

jedes Jahr; einen zehntägigen Urlaub; dieses Jahr; einer der Glücklichen; unsere Schulgruppe; mit großer Begeisterung; in einem reizenden Berggasthof.

2) HAUPTTEIL

Endlich kam der Tag der Abfahrt. Die Busreise war lang und ermüdend, aber beim imposanten Anblick der schneebedeckten Berge war sie schnell vergessen.

Bei herrlichem Wetter fuhren wir täglich Schi, was auch mir als Anfänger viel Spaß machte. Es war doch recht lustig, die Pisten hinunterzufahren, ohne bremsen zu können! [50 words]

ANALYSIS

1. Use of cases

Nominative: *der Tag; die Reise*

Accusative: *viel Spaß; die Pisten*

Genitive: *der Abfahrt; der schneebedeckten Berge*

Dative: *beim imposanten Anblick; bei herrlichem Wetter; mir . . . Spaß machte*

2. Use of verbs

Notice the use of the separable verb *Schi fahren* and the expression *jemandem Spaß machen*.

There are also two dependent infinitive phrases: *die Pisten hinunterzufahren; ohne bremsen zu können.*

3. Sentence structure

There are three instances of inversion of subject and verb, a subordinate clause introduced by *was*, and two dependent infinitive phrases (see 2 above). All these demonstrate a command of word order.

4. Use of vocabulary

The atmosphere of the *Einleitung* is maintained by the use of such expressions as *beim imposanten Anblick; bei herrlichem Wetter; viel Spaß; recht lustig.*

Mastery of the rules of adjective agreement is shown by the use of correct endings on *imposant, schneebedeckt* and *herrlich* when the adjective comes before the noun and by the absence of endings on *lang* and *ermüdend* when the adjective comes after the noun.

The use of the particle *doch* and the adverb *recht* shows familiarity with the everyday use of 'real' German.

3) SCHLUSS

> Der Urlaub war wirklich fabelhaft gewesen, aber es hat alles einmal ein Ende. Am letzten Morgen packte ich schweren Herzens meine Sachen in den Koffer ein und machte mich zur Abreise bereit. Als der Bus ankam, warf ich einen letzten Blick auf die atemberaubende Landschaft, die mir so imponiert hatte. „Ich komme wieder!" versprach ich mir.   [56 words]

ANALYSIS

1. Use of cases

Nominative: *der Urlaub; der Bus*

Accusative: *ein Ende; meine Sachen; in den Koffer; mich; einen letzten Blick; die ... Landschaft*

Genitive: *schweren Herzens*

Dative: *am letzten Morgen; zur Abreise; mir imponiert; versprach ich mir*

2. Use of verbs

Notice the variety of verb use: two separable verbs (*einpacken, ankommen*); a reflexive verb (*sich bereit machen*), and two verbs taking the dative (*imponieren, versprechen*). Although the imperfect tense is used mostly, the pluperfect tense occurs twice: *war ... gewesen; ...imponiert hatte.*

3. Sentence structure

The sentence beginning *Als der Bus ankam ...* shows an ability to use complex clause structures. First, there is a subordinate clause which is followed by a main clause, and then immediately after, there follows a relative clause beginning with *die.*

There is also an example of inversion of subject and verb in this paragraph: *packte ich.*

4. Use of vocabulary

It is important that the essay does not fizzle out in a disappointing anti-climax. Notice how it finishes on a positive note – *Ich komme wieder!* – despite the tone of sadness in this last part.

Again, avoid a bare account of facts; try to put across feelings and reactions. This has been done here through the use of: *wirklich fabelhaft, schweren Herzens, atemberaubende Landschaft, imponiert* and *Ich komme wieder!*

Considerable use has been made of adjectives, not only to create atmosphere, but also to show understanding of the rules of adjective agreement. Thus, we find *am letzten Morgen, schweren Herzens, einen letzten Blick, die atemberaubende Landschaft* as examples of adjectives preceding the noun, and *fabelhaft* as an example of an adjective following the noun.

Notice the use of the idiomatic expression, *es hat alles einmal ein Ende.*

4) THE COMPLETE MODEL

QUESTION – Write in German an essay of about 150 words describing a school ski trip to Austria or Switzerland.

PLAN – *Osterferien — zehn Tage — Schulgruppe — Alpen — Berggasthof — Reise — Wetter — Schi fahren — Spaß — lustig — Abreise — schweren Herzens*

ESSAY – *Unser Deutschlehrer organisierte jedes Jahr in den Oster-ferien einen zehntägigen Schiurlaub in Österreich. Dieses Jahr war ich einer der Glücklichen, die einen Platz bekamen. Unsere Schulgruppe bestand aus dreißig Teilnehmern, die sich monatelang mit großer Begeisterung auf den Aufenthalt in einem reizenden Berggasthof hoch in den Alpen gefreut hatten.*

Endlich kam der Tag der Abfahrt. Die Busreise war lang und ermüdend, aber beim imposanten Anblick der schneebedeckten Berge war sie schnell vergessen.

Bei herrlichem Wetter fuhren wir täglich Schi, was auch mir als Anfänger viel Spaß machte. Es war doch recht lustig, die Pisten hinunterzufahren, ohne bremsen zu können!

Der Urlaub war wirklich fabelhaft gewesen, aber es hat alles einmal ein Ende. Am letzten Morgen packte ich schweren Herzens meine Sachen in den Koffer ein und machte mich zur Abreise bereit. Als der Bus ankam, warf ich einen letzten Blick auf die atemberaubende Landschaft, die mir so imponiert hatte. „Ich komme wieder!" versprach ich mir.   [155 words]

C | SINGLE-TOPIC ESSAY PRACTICE

In all the essays below, you should use about 150 words of German, although this may vary a little, depending on which examination you are preparing for.

Content

Remember:

* Plan your essay first: jot down some key phrases you wish to use.

* Make sure your command of German vocabulary and grammar is good enough for the essay you want to write (if not, write something different).

* Don't use up too many words on one part of the story.

* Don't just list bare facts, but share your feelings and reactions as well – if you are working from your imagination, think how you would feel and what you would do if it really happened to you.

Structure

Remember:

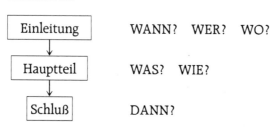

Einleitung	WANN? WER? WO?
Hauptteil	WAS? WIE?
Schluß	DANN?

Suggested vocabulary can be found in the Language Resource Bank at the back of the book.

1	Write an essay in German about a day spent with a friend whom you have not seen for two years.

In this essay, try particularly to:

* use the pluperfect tense (see Chapter One, section B.2, p.4).

* introduce conversation with at least four verbs in the perfect tense (see Chapter One, section B.2, p.4).

* use three relative clauses.

2	Write an essay in German about a visit to the shops one day during the week before Christmas.

In this essay, try particularly to:

* follow the Time–Manner–Place (WANN?–WIE?–WO?) rule (see Chapter One, section B.2, p.5).

* use some exclamations (Language Resource Bank, section A.3).

* use one synonym for each of *glücklich, unglücklich, zornig, sagen* (L.R.B., section B.1).

3	Write an essay in German about a day that you found particularly disappointing.

In this essay, try particularly to:

* use at least two clauses beginning with *als* and *nachdem* (Language Resource Bank, section A.6, "Explanation links").

* use an idiom expressing **Surprise** (L.R.B., section C.8).

* use a synonym for *schlecht* and a synonym for *unglücklich* (L.R.B., section B.1).

4	Write an essay in German about an unusual day at your school.

In this essay, try particularly to:

* use an adjective that expresses the unusual (Language Resource Bank, part (ix) of section B.1).

* use an idiom to do with **Humour, ridicule** or with **Rebukes** (L.R.B., section C.6 or C.7).

* use the common particles *schon* and *nur* (L.R.B., section B.2).

5	Write an essay in German about someone you greatly admire.

In this essay, try particularly to:

* use two synonyms for *gut* (Language Resource Bank, section B.1).

* show your mastery of the rules of adjective agreement (see Chapter One, section B.2, p.5).

* use two subordinate clauses introduced by *weil* and *da* (L.R.B., section A.6, "Explanation links").

6	Write a composition using the title: *Ein Besuch beim Arzt.*

In this essay, try particularly to:

* use synonyms for *schlecht, unglücklich* and *sagen* (Language Resource Bank, section B.1).

* use the particles *eben* and *wohl* (L.R.B., section B.2).

* use some interesting **Feelings and reactions** vocabulary (L.R.B., section A.2).

7	Write a composition using the title: *Eine Reise ins Ausland.*

In this essay, try particularly to:

* use some interesting **Feelings and reactions** vocabulary (Language Resource Bank, section A.2).

* use some time links (L.R.B., section A.6).

* use three clauses introduced by *nachdem, während* and *kaum* (L.R.B., section A.6, "Explanation links").

8	Write a composition using the title: *Ein Abend im Theater.*

In this essay, try particularly to:

* use two synonyms for *gut* and two for *schlecht* (Language Resource Bank, section B.1).

* use the particles *etwa* and *ja* (L.R.B., section B.2).

* use some appropriate exclamations (L.R.B., section A.3).

9	Write a composition using the title: *Meine Lieblingsstadt.*

In this essay, try particularly to:

* show your mastery of the rules of adjective agreement (see Chapter One, section B.2, p.5).

* use synonyms for *groß,. gut,* and an adjective that expresses the unusual (Language Resource Bank, section B.1).

* show your mastery of cases (see Chapter One, section B.2, p.3).

10	Write a composition using the title: *Ein interessanter Ferienjob.*

In this essay, try particularly to:

* use some interesting **Activity, behaviour** vocabulary (Language Resource Bank, section A.4).

* use some interesting **Feelings and reactions** vocabulary (L.R.B., section A.2).

* use three relative clauses.

11	*Beschreiben Sie eine Fernseh- oder Radiosendung, die Ihnen besonders gefällt.*

In this essay, try particularly to:

* use some interesting **Feelings and reactions** vocabulary (Language Resource Bank, section A.2).

* use the particles *doch* and *mal* (L.R.B., section B.2).

* show your mastery of the rules of adjective agreement (see Chapter One, section B.2, p.5).

12	*Beschreiben Sie einen Tag, an dem Sie viel Angst hatten.*

In this essay, try particularly to:

* use some interesting **Feelings and reactions** vocabulary (Language Resource Bank, section A.2).

* use an idiom of **Despair** or **Fear** (L.R.B., section C.1 or C.4).

* use clauses introduced by *als, kaum* and *um . . . zu* (L.R.B., section A.6, "Explanation links").

13 *Beschreiben Sie einige deutsche Feste und Feiertage.*

In this essay, try particularly to:

* use some time links (Language Resource Bank, section A.6).

* use three clauses introduced by *nachdem, während, als* (L.R.B., section A.6).

* show your mastery of the rules of adjective agreement (see Chapter One, section B.2, p.5).

14 *Erzählen Sie von einem Urlaub, den Sie auf einem Campingplatz verbracht haben.*

In this essay, try particularly to:

* use some interesting **Feelings and reactions** vocabulary (Language Resource Bank, section A.2).

* use appropriate time links (L.R.B., section A.6).

* use synonyms for *gut* and *schlecht* (L.R.B., section B.1).

15 *Sie waren Augenzeuge/Augenzeugin bei einem Verkehrsunfall. Schreiben Sie für die Polizei einen ausführlichen Bericht darüber.*

In this essay, try particularly to:

* use some appropriate **Feelings and reactions** vocabulary (Language Resource Bank, section A.2).

* use some appropriate **Activity, behaviour** vocabulary (L.R.B., section A.4).

* use time links and explanation links (L.R.B., section A.6).

Part Three

LETTERS

INTRODUCTORY NOTES

1.   Notes on how to write letters are followed by models for various types of letter coupled with exercises – two to each type of letter.

2.   150 words was chosen as a useful working number for model letters as this is a typical requirement in Certificate examinations. Your own particular examination may, however, require fewer words. To gain an idea of how a model letter of fewer words would look, reduce or omit portions of the printed model letters as required. If you were required to use a little more than 150 words, only an extra two or three lines would need to be added to the printed model letters.

3.   There is no analysis of grammar or vocabulary of the model letters. As the principles involved are the same as for essay writing, it might be helpful to refer back to the analyses of model essays in previous chapters, which point to what is looked for in writing generally.

4.   There are altogether 20 letter writing tasks.

5.   The tasks are chosen to reflect those which regularly occur in external examinations.

6.   The length of the exercises can be varied as required. The suggested lengths are merely guidelines.

7.   The exercises could be carried out orally prior to being written.

8.   The grammar suggestions are designed to be easily incorporated in the particular letter task to which they are attached.

9.   The basic vocabulary required for each exercise is broadly contained in the model letters. Only for the first letter is additional vocabulary given, because of the diversity of possible answers.

5
Writing Letters

1) *DIE ANREDE* – THE FORM OF ADDRESS

When beginning a letter in German, translate 'Dear' as shown in the table below.

INFORMAL

MASCULINE	FEMININE
Lieber Josef!	Liebe Hilde!
Lieber Opa!	Liebe Oma!
Lieber Onkel Hans! [Instead of *Liebe(r)* one can use *Hallo*, and in Austria *Servus*, which are even more informal]	Liebe Tante Rosa!

PLURAL

Meine Lieben! (Dear all)

Meine lieben Eltern!

Liebe Maria, lieber Walter! (Feminine usually precedes masculine)

FORMAL

MASCULINE	FEMININE	NEUTER
Lieber Herr Gruber!	Liebe Frau Gruber!	Liebes Fräulein Gruber!
(If the above are personally known)		
Sehr geehrter Herr Gruber!	Sehr geehrte Frau Gruber!	Sehr geehrtes Fräulein Gruber!
(If the above are **not** personally known)		
Sehr geehrter Herr Direktor!	Sehr geehrte Frau Direktor!	Sehr geehrtes Fräulein Studienrat!
(If addressing people by their title)		

Sehr geehrte Herren!
(If writing to a company, office, agency, etc.)

Liebe Familie Schmidt!

Liebe Frau Holzer, lieber Herr Holzer!
(Feminine usually precedes masculine)

2) USE OF CAPITAL LETTERS

The pronouns *Du, Ihr,* and their respective possessive adjectives (*Dein, Euer,* etc.) are always written with capitals when writing letters.

3) *DIE SCHLUSSFORMEL* – SIGNING OFF

The table below shows you how to sign off, i.e. how to say 'Best wishes', 'Yours sincerely', etc.

INFORMAL		FORMAL	
Viele Grüße		*Mit freundlichen Grüßen*	
Herzliche Grüße		*Mit freundlichem Gruß*	Yours sincerely
Herzlichst	Best wishes	*Mit bestem Gruß*	(to people)
Mit herzlichen Grüßen		*Mit den besten Grüßen*	
		Hochachtungsvoll	Yours faithfully
Liebe Grüße	Love	*Mit vorzüglicher Hochachtung*	(to companies etc.)
Alles Liebe			

The above are followed by

Dein/Deine + name(s)	*Ihr/Ihre* + name(s)
Euer/Eure + name(s)	

(N.B. The name can also be positioned **beneath** *Dein/Euer Ihr,* etc.)

4) THE LAYOUT

a) ADDRESS AND DATE – The Germans do not write the full address at the head of a letter: They simply write the name of the town followed by a comma, then the date. This appears at top right. (The full address of the sender is written on the back of the envelope.) The date is preceded by *den.* The number comes next, followed by a full stop, then the month. A typical date heading would look like this:

Hamburg, den 9. März

b) *DIE ANREDE* – You may choose whether you indent the *Anrede* away from the margin or not, although in formal letters it is usual not to. It is followed by either an exclamation mark or a comma. The opening line of the letter begins with a capital letter if an exclamation mark is used with the *Anrede*, a small letter if a comma follows the *Anrede*.

A typical opening might be:

> Stratford-upon-Avon, der 24. April
>
> Lieber Helmut!
>
> Ich habe Deine Adresse von unserer deutschen Sprachassistentin bekommen.

Notice that there is a gap between the *Anrede* and the first line. Although this is not obligatory, it is quite common practice.

Another way of writing the above would be:

> Stratford-upon-Avon, der 24. April
>
> Lieber Helmut,
>
> ich habe Deine Adresse von unserer deutscher Sprachassistentin bekommen.

Notice how the opening line begins with a small letter because *Lieber Helmut* has been followed by a comma, not an exclamation mark.

c) PARAGRAPHS – In formal letters, the first line of a new paragraph is not usually indented. In informal letters you are free to choose whether you indent or start against the left margin.

It is often the practice to leave a line between paragraphs, especially when no indenting has occurred.

d) *DIE SCHLUSSFORMEL* — *This is positioned at the foot of the letter, usually on the right-hand side or in the middle of the page. An example would be:*

> Ich danke Ihnen im voraus für
> Ihre Auskunft.
>
> Mit freundlichen Grüßen
> Ihr
> Kurt Müller

or

> Ich freue mich auf Deinen Besuch. Schreib bald
> wieder.
>
> Herzliche Grüße
>
> Dein
>
> Peter

N.B. After *Mit freundlichen Grüßen, Herzliche Grüße* etc. you may put a comma, but it is not obligatory.

5) STYLE

Obviously your style will depend on whether your letter is informal or formal. In the former, colloquial expressions and exclamations are acceptable, but not in the latter. Formal letters tend to be matter-of-fact and businesslike, so do not include 'chatty' language.

See Chapter One, section B for an in-depth discussion of writing style.

6) CONTENT

Always **follow closely** the instructions given. Do not be tempted to include irrelevant material you have learned by heart in the hope of a better mark – or to repeat yourself if you run out of vocabulary or ideas. Either of these will have the opposite result to what you want, as it will show up a poor command of German and a lack of creative writing ability.

1 | INTRODUCING YOURSELF

Stratford-upon-Avon, den 4. April

Lieber Helmut!

Ich habe Deine Adresse von unserer Sprachassistentin bekommen und freue mich sehr, einen Briefwechsel mit Dir beginnen zu können.

Ich heiße Peter Smith und werde am zweiten August sechzehn Jahre alt. Ich werde meinen Geburtstag dieses Jahr wahrscheinlich auf Urlaub in Wales verbringen. Ich habe eine achtzehnjährige Schwester Mary, die bei einer Computer-Firma angestellt ist.

Beigelegt ist eine Aufnahme von mir, die neulich bei uns im Garten gemacht worden ist. Ich bin begeisterter Sportler, vor allem mag ich Squash. Kennst Du dieser Sport? Ich lese gern und höre gern Musik, aber mein spezielles Hobby ist Briefmarkensammeln. In der Schule ist mein Lieblingsfach Geographie.

Mein Vater ist Frauenarzt und ist in der Birmighamer Universitäts-Klinik tätig. Meine Mutter ist Hausfrau, war aber früher Krankenschwester. Wir wohnen in einem Einzelhaus in Stratford, einer reizenden mittelalterlichen Stadt in Mittelengland.

Ich freue mich sehr auf baldige Antwort.

Herzliche Grüße

Dein

Peter

[151 words]

A Study the letter carefully, then write to a new German pen-friend, giving him/her the following information in about 150 words of German. You will find the vocabulary you need in the letter, in the Language Resource Bank at the back of the book and – for this exercise only – on the following pages.

1. You got his/her address from your German teacher
2. You are pleased to be able to start writing to him/her
3. Your name and date of birth
4. Where you will be spending your birthday this year
5. The age and occupation of your brother(s) and sister(s)
6. You are enclosing a recent photo of yourself
7. You are keen on sport
8. You like reading and listening to music
9. Your particular hobby
10. Your favourite subject at school
11. Your father's and your mother's occupation
12. The house you live in
13. The town in which you live
14. You are looking forward to an early reply

———————————————

B Imagine Helmut's reply to Peter. In about 150 words, he tells Peter:

1. His age and date of birth
2. The age and occupation of his 20-year-old brother
3. That he is enclosing a recent photograph of himself
4. That he does not like sport
5. That his hobby is computers
6. That he enjoys watching T.V. and going to the cinema
7. That his favourite subject at school is Maths
8. His father's and mother's occupation
9. That he lives in a terraced house in an industrial city
10. That he hopes that he and Peter will be able to meet

Write this letter and try to make reference to the specific points listed. Also try particularly to:

* show your mastery of the rules of adjective agreement (see Chapter One, section B.2, p.5).

* use two relative clauses (as in the model letter)

* use two subordinate clauses introduced by *da* (Language Resource Bank, section A.6, "Explanation links") and *wo*.

Special Vocabulary for 'Introducing Yourself'

Types of home

der Bauernhof	– farm
der Bungalow	– bungalow
das Doppelhaus	– semi-detached house
das Einfamilienhaus	– detached house
das Einzelhaus	– detached house
das Reihenhaus	– terraced house
der Wohnblock	– block of flats
die Wohnung	– flat

Locations

See Language Resource Bank, section A.1, part (iii)

also:

im Norden	– in the north
im Süden	– in the south
im Osten	– in the east
im Westen	– in the west
im Nordosten	– in the north-east

im Nordwesten	– in the north-west
im Südosten	– in the south-east
im Südwesten	– in the south-west
in der Mitte von	– in the centre of
in der Nähe von	– near

Occupations

der Angestellte	– employee, clerk
der Apotheker	– chemist
der Arbeiter	– labourer
der Arzt	– doctor
der Bankier	– banker
der Bauer	– farmer
der Bergarbeiter	– miner
der Briefträger	– postman
der Hafenarbeiter	– docker
der Ingenieur	– engineer
der Kaufmann	– businessman
der Krämer	– shopkeeper
die Krankenschwester	– nurse
der Lehrer	– teacher
der Lkw-Fahrer	– lorry driver
der Postbeamte	– post-office clerk
die Sekretärin	– secretary
die Stenotypistin	– typist
der Vertreter	– representative

Hobbies

Ausflüge machen	– going on trips
basteln	– making things
Kino/Theaterbesuche	– cinema/theatre visits
Musik hören/machen	– listening to/making music
etwas sammeln	– collecting things
Sport treiben	– doing sport
stricken	– knitting
Vögel beobachten	– bird-watching
wandern	– hiking
zeichnen	– drawing

London, den 20. Juni

Liebe Hilde!

Ich freue mich sehr, daß Du in den Sommerferien zwei Wochen bei uns verbringen willst. Ich bin sicher, daß es Dir hier gut gefallen wird.

Wann und wie willst Du hierher kommen? Meine Eltern möchten Deine genaue Ankunftszeit wissen, damit wir Dich abholen können. An welchem Tag mußt Du abreisen?

Leider mußt Du mit mir ein Zimmer teilen, weil wir nicht genug Platz haben, um Dir Dein eigenes Zimmer anbieten zu können. Ich hoffe, daß Du nichts dagegen hast.

Gibt es etwas, was Du nicht gern ißt? Wenn Du etwas besonders gern essen möchtest, da brauchst Du es nur zu sagen, und meine Mutter wird es kochen.

In London können wir viel unternehmen. Welche Sehenswürdigkeiten möchtest Du am liebsten sehen? Gehst Du gern in Museen und Kunstgalerien? Wenn Du Lust dazu hast, können wir uns die vielen schönen Geschäfte ansehen.

Bitte schreib bald wieder.

Viele herzliche Grüße

Deine

Karen

[151 words]

A Study the letter carefully, then write in about 150 words a similar letter to a German pen-friend who is shortly to visit you. In particular ask him/her:

1. How and when (s)he intends to travel

2. When (s)he must depart

3. If (s)he would mind sharing a room

4. If there is anything (s)he particularly likes to eat

5. What (s)he would like to do during his/her stay

In this letter, try particularly to:

* use two subordinate clauses with *wenn* and *daß* (as in the model letter).

* show mastery of the Time–Manner–Place (WANN?–WIE?–WO?) rule (see Chapter One, section B.2, p.5).

* use either an *um . . . zu* or a *damit* construction (as in the model letter).

B Imagine you are Karen replying to this letter. In about 150 words, include the following information in your letter.

1. Your exact date and time of arrival

2. The date of your departure

3. You do not mind sharing a room

4. What you particularly like and dislike eating

5. The sights you would like to see

6. Whether you like museums and art galleries

7. Whether you would like to see the shops

In this letter, try particularly to:

* use the particles *wohl* and *doch* (Language Resource Bank, section B.2).

* use subordinate clauses introduced by *weil* and *wenn* (as in the model letter).

* show mastery of the rules of adjective agreement (see Chapter One, section B.2, p.5).

3 THANKS FOR HOSPITALITY

Reading, den 25. August

Liebe Familie Sasshofer!

Ich bin am Dienstagabend gut angekommen. Die Reise war recht angenehm, obgleich ich mich auf der Überfahrt etwas krank fühlte, weil die See sehr stürmisch war. Meine Eltern haben mich in London vom Bahnhof abgeholt und dann nach Reading gefahren.

Ich möchte mich für Ihre Gastfreundschaft herzlich bedanken. Die Zeit, die ich bei Ihnen im Rheinland verbracht habe, war wirklich großartig. Es ist kaum zu glauben, daß wir in nur zwei Wochen so viel unternommen haben. Die Rheinfahrt hat ein großen Eindruck auf mich gemacht, besonders die herrliche Strecke zwischen Bonn und Mainz. Auch die Lorelei werde ich immer in Erinnerung behalten, nicht nur wegen der schönen Aussicht von oben, sondern auch wegen des anstrengenden Aufstiegs!

Ich bin Ihnen dankbar, Frau Sasshofer, daß Sie mir eine so große Auswahl an Gerichten angeboten haben. Das deutsche Essen hat köstlich geschmeckt!

Nochmals vielen herzlichen Dank für alles.
Mit den besten Grüßen
Ihr Michael

[153 words]

A Study the letter carefully, then write in about 150 words a similar letter to the parents of your German pen-friend. In particular tell them:

1. About your journey home

2. That you were met at the station by your parents

3. That you are grateful for their hospitality

4. That you really enjoyed the time you spent with them

5. What in particular made a big impression on you

6. About something else that you will always remember

7. What you thought about German food

In this letter, try particularly to:

* use three subordinate clauses with *weil, daß* and *obgleich* (as in the model letter).

* show mastery of the perfect tense.

* use a relative clause (as in the model letter).

B In about 150 words, write a letter to a friend telling him/her about a holiday you have just spent with a German family. In particular tell him/her:

1. How you travelled there

2. That you were met at the airport/station

3. About your first impression of Germany on arrival

4. The sights that you saw

5. About something that you will particularly remember

6. What you thought about German food

7. That you were grateful for your hosts' hospitality

In this letter, try particularly to:

* show mastery of the perfect tense.

* use three subordinate clauses with *weil, daß* and *obgleich* (as in the model letter)

* use synonyms for *gut, glücklich* and *groß* (Language Resource Bank, section B.1).

Chester, den 15. März

Lieber Walter,

kurz nach Weihnachten sind wir nach Chester übersiedelt, weil mein Vater seine Stellung gewechselt hat. Der Umzug in unsere neue Wohnung ist reibungslos verlaufen, und wir haben uns hier schon gut eingelebt.

Chester liegt in Nordwestengland etwa dreißig Kilometer von Liverpool entfernt und hat ungefähr 70 000 Einwohner. Es ist eine reizende mittelalterliche Stadt mit einer Menge alter Fachwerkhäuser.

Die Stadt ist berühmt für ihre Geschäftsreihen, die in zwei Etagen übereinander gebaut sind. Auch sehenswert sind die Kathedrale, deren Architektur die Zeit vom zwölften bis zum neunzehnten Jahrhundert umspannt, die alte Stadtmauer, die Burg, das neugotische Rathaus, die römischen Überreste und der Zoo, der der zweitgrößte Englands ist. Es gibt auch einen Pferderennplatz und ein Fußballstadion, wo Chester City in der englischen Nationalliga spielt. Auf der Dee kann man Flußfahrten machen oder ein Ruderboot mieten.

Komm uns mal besuchen. Es gefällt Dir ganz bestimmt hier!

Viele Grüße
Dein
John

[152 words]

A Study the letter carefully, then write in about 150 words a similar letter that you have received from your German pen-friend who has recently moved to another town. In particular, your pen-pal tells you the following:

1. That his/her father has changed his job

2. That the family moved house after Christmas/Easter

3. That they have settled into their new home

4. In which part of Germany their new home is situated

5. How many inhabitants live in the town they have moved to

6. The kind of town it is – medieval, industrial etc.

7. At least 5 sights that can be visited

8. That you ought to come to visit him as you would like it there

In this letter, try particularly to:

* show your mastery of the rules of adjective agreement (see Chapter One, section B.2, p.5).

* use two relative clauses (as in the model letter).

* use three nouns in the accusative case.

B Write a letter to your German pen-friend, telling him/her that you have recently moved to another town. In this letter compare the town you have moved to with the town you have left in about 150 words. In particular, make reference to:

1. The difference in geographical location

2. The difference in size

3. The contrast in the sights

In this letter, try particularly to:

* show mastery of the rules of adjective agreement (see Chapter One, section B.2, p.5).

* use the particles *doch, ja* and *wohl* (Language Resource Bank, section B.2).

* use synonyms for *groß, gut* and *schlecht* and an adjective to express the unusual (L.R.B., section B.1).

DESCRIBING YOUR SUMMER HOLIDAY

Manchester, den 16. September

Liebe Eva!

Bitte entschuldige, daß ich Deinen netten Brief erst jetzt beantworte. Leider hat die Vorbereitung auf die Schulprüfung meine Zeit völlig in Anspruch genommen.

Wie geht es Dir? Wie hast Du die Sommerferien verbracht? Mit meinen Eltern und meinem Bruder war ich zehn Tage in Wales. Wir haben in einem netten Wohnwagen an der See gewohnt.

Am ersten Tag unseres Urlaubs haben wir die Burg zu Caernarfon besichtigt, wo die feierliche Investitur von Prinz Charles stattfand. Diese Burg ist fast vollständig erhalten, und sie wirkt echt mächtig.

Weil das Wetter einfach prächtig war, sind wir viel in der See geschwommen. Auch sind wir in die Berge wandern gegangen oder zum Picknick gefahren. Der Höhepunkt des Urlaubs – nicht nur buchstäblich! – war der Aufstieg zum Gipfel des Snowdon. Unsere Eltern waren auch oben, sind jedoch mit der Bergbahn hinaufgefahren!

Hoffentlich geht es Dir gut. Schreib mir doch von Deinen Sommerferien!

Herzlichst
Deine
Julie

[151 words]

A Study the letter carefully, then in about 150 words write to your German pen-friend to apologise for not having replied to his/her letter, and to tell him/her about your recent holiday away with your family. In particular, try to mention the following:

1. That you are sorry for taking so long to reply

2. A reason for the delay in writing

3. Where you went with your family

4. How long you were away

5. Where you stayed

6. What the weather was like

7. What you did

In this letter, try particularly to:

✱ follow the Time–Manner–Place (WANN?–WIE?–WO?) rule (see Chapter One, section B.2, p.5).

✱ show mastery of the perfect tense.

✱ use all four cases.

B Imagine you are Eva replying to Julie. In about 150 words, try to mention the following points in your letter:

1. That you are pleased Julie enjoyed her holiday

2. That you would also like to visit Wales

3. Why you would like to visit Wales

4. Where you spent your summer holiday

5. How long you were away

6. Where you stayed

7. What the weather was like

8. What you did

In this letter, try particularly to:

✱ follow the Time–Manner–Place (WANN?–WIE?–WO?) rule (see Chapter One, section B.2, p.5).

✱ show mastery of the perfect tense.

✱ use all four cases.

Birmingham, den 9. Februar

Lieber Gerhard,

damit Du genügend Informationen über das englische Schulleben für Deinen Aufsatz hast, beschreibe ich Dir jetzt den Verlauf eines typischen Schultags in unserer Schule.

Um Viertel vor neun gehe ich zur Garderobe, um meinen Mantel abzulegen, dann gehe ich ins Klassenzimmer, wo unser Klassenvorstand kontrolliert, wer heute fehlt. Gleich danach gibt es die Morgenandacht im Versammlungssaal.

Der Morgenunterricht beginnt um Viertel nach neun. Im Laufe des Tags gibt es acht Schulstunden, je von fünfunddreißig Minuten Dauer. Morgens und nachmittags gibt es zwei kurze Pausen. In der einstündigen Mittagspause ißt man entweder zu Hause oder im Speisesaal.

Ich nehme vier Pflichtfächer - Englisch, Mathematik, Religion, und Sport - und sechs Wahlfächer mit Schwerpunkt Naturwissenschaften und Fremdsprachen. Samstags gibt es keinen Unterricht wie bei Euch, aber abends müssen wir viele Hausaufgaben machen.

Hoffentlich ist Dir diese Beschreibung behilflich. Ich drücke Dir die Daumen, daß Du eine Eins bekommst !

Viele herzliche Grüße
Dein
Steven

[150 words]

A Your pen-friend has requested information that would be useful for a talk he/she has to give on English school life. Write a letter of about 150 words, in which you state the following:

1. You are going to describe a typical day at your school

2. The time you arrive at school

3. That you first of all go to the cloakroom

4. That you then go to registration

5. That there is a morning assembly

6. The time the first lesson begins

7. How many lessons you have each day

8. How long each lesson lasts

9. How many breaks you have during the day

10. What happens at lunchtime

11. The subjects that you study

12. That there is no school on Saturday

13. How much homework you have

14. You hope your information has been helpful

In this letter, try particularly to:

* use all four cases.

* use clauses beginning with *um . . . zu, wo* and *daß* (as in the model letter).

* invert subject and verb at least 5 times.

B You are required to write an essay about a typical day in a German school. In about 150 words, write to your pen-friend requesting the following information:

1. The time (s)he arrives at school

2. What (s)he has to do on arrival

3. Is there registration?

4. Is there a morning assembly?

5. The time the first lesson begins

6. How long each lesson lasts

7. How many lessons there are per day

8. How many breaks there are per day

9. What happens at lunch time?

10. What subjects (s)he studies

11. Whether there is school at lunchtime

12. The amount of homework that is given and when it has to be done

In this letter, try particularly to:

* use linking expressions to avoid a tedious list of questions (see Language Resource Bank, section A.6).

* use all four cases.

* use clauses beginning with *damit* and *wo* (as in the model letter).

7 WRITING ABOUT YOUR BIRTHDAY

Guildford, den 4. Oktober

Liebe Christl,

es war sehr lieb von Dir, mir das schöne Geschenk zu meinem Geburtstag zu schicken. Die Holzschnitzerei ist wirklich nett, und ich freue mich sehr, etwas echt Schweizerisches zu haben. Vielen herzlichen Dank dafür.

Von meinen Eltern habe ich eine neue elegante Handtasche aus Leder bekommen, und von meiner Schwester die neueste Langspielplatte von Cliff Richard. Ich mag seine Musik wahnsinnig gern. Ist er bei Euch in der Schweiz auch beliebt?

Weil dieses Jahr mein Geburtstag auf einen Samstag gefallen ist, haben mir meine Eltern eine besondere Freude gemacht und mich zum Hockey-Länderspiel England gegen Schottland im Wembley-Stadion eingeladen. Das Spiel war irrsinnig gut.

Am Abend ist es auch recht lustig zugegangen, denn wir haben eine tolle Party veranstaltet, zu der viele meiner Klassenkameradinnen und Kameraden gekommen sind. Obgleich das Wohnzimmer zum Bersten voll war, haben wir viel Spaß beim Tanzen gehabt.

Nochmals vielen Dank für Dein Geschenk.

Herzlichst
Deine Angela

[153 words]

A Study the letter carefully then write a similar letter to your pen-friend in about 150 words. Be sure to include the following points:

1. Your thanks for the present (s)he sent you

2. What you thought about the present

3. What presents you received from members of your family

4. How you spent the day

5. How you spent the evening

In this letter, try particularly to:

* show mastery of the perfect tense.

* use two sentences in which a subordinate clause precedes a main clause (as in the model letter).

* use a verb taking the dative.

B Imagine you are Christl replying to Angela. In about 150 words, tell her:

1. That you are pleased Angela liked the present

2. That Cliff Richard is quite popular in Switzerland

3. That you don't think his music is bad, but that you personally prefer X

4. That you didn't know Angela liked hockey, and that you would like to know if she plays it at school

5. That you recently went to a party which you didn't enjoy because it was too crowded and because the music was bad

In this letter, try particularly to:

* use subordinate clauses with *weil* and *obgleich* (as in the model letter).

* use a verb taking the dative.

* use the particles *ja* and *doch* (Language Resource Bank, section B.2).

Cardiff, den 14. April

Fremdenverkehrsverband Telfs
Untermarktstraße
A-6410 Telfs/Tirol

Sehr geehrte Herren,

für den August dieses Jahres habe ich die Absicht, mit meiner Frau und meinen Kindern Urlaub in Tirol zu machen. Ich bitte Sie daher, mir eine Liste der Hotels und Pensionen möglichst mit Preisangabe für Halb- und Vollpension zuzusenden. Ich bitte Sie auch um einen Ortsplan und um Prospektmaterial über Sehenswürdigkeiten und Ausflugsziele, die besonders empfehlenswert sind.

Würden Sie mir auch Informationen über die Unterhaltungsmöglichkeiten für Kinder senden? Gibt es zum Beispiel ein Frei- oder Hallenbad oder sonstige Sporteinrichtungen, die für Kinder geeignet sind?

Weil wir mit der Bahn fahren, möchte ich während unseres Aufenthalts ein Auto mieten. Gibt es in Telfs oder in der näheren Umgebung einen Autoverleih? Wenn nicht, würden Sie mir Auskunft über Buslinien senden, eventuell auch einen Fahrplan für die Linie Telfs-Innsbruck? Kann man ermäßigte Fahrkarten für Touristen oder Familien bekommen?

Ich danke Ihnen im voraus für Ihre Bemühungen
Hochachtungsvoll
Peter Williams

[151 words]

A   Imagine you are your father writing to the tourist information office in a German town. In a letter of 150 words:

1. State when you will be coming, and who is accompanying you

2. Ask for a list of hotels and guesthouses with the price for half board and full board

3. Ask for a town plan

4. Ask for brochures with information about the sights and recommended excursions

5. Enquire about entertainment for children

6. Enquire about sports facilities

7. Ask about the possibility of car hire

8. Ask for information about bus services and whether there are special reductions for tourists and families

9. Thank the office for their trouble

In this letter, try particularly to:

* use two relative clauses (as in the model letter).

* use a subordinate clauses with *weil* (as in the model letter).

* follow the Time–Manner–Place (WANN?–WIE?–WO?) rule (see Chapter One, section B.2, p.5).

_____

B Imagine you and a friend are going to spend a camping holiday in Germany in the summer. Write to the tourist information office in the nearest town in about 150 words and ask for the following:

1. A town map

2. Information about sights, excursions and special events that are on while you are there

3. Information about sports and other outdoor activities (hiking, climbing, riding, etc.)

4. Information about public transport (buses, trains, trams)

5. Whether there are special rates for students on public transport, in swimming pools, sports centres, cinemas etc.

6. Whether you need to bring a student identity card

In this letter, try particularly to:

* use all four cases.

* use two relative clauses (as in the model letter).

* use a subordinate clause with *wann* (as in the model letter) – also one with *ob*.

BOOKING ACCOMMODATION IN A HOTEL OR GUESTHOUSE

Cardiff, den 2. Mai

An die Direktion
Berggasthof Lehen
Lehen 3
A-6410 Telfs/Tirol

Sehr geehrte Herren,

ich möchte gerne mit meiner Frau und meinen zwei Kindern zwei Wochen im August bei Ihnen verbringen. Ich wäre Ihnen sehr dankbar, wenn Sie mir ein Doppelzimmer und zwei Einzelzimmer für die Zeit vom 1. August (Anreisetag) bis zum 14. August (Abreisetag) reservieren würden. Wenn möglich, hätten wir am liebsten Zimmer mit Balkon und Blick auf die Berge. Die Zimmer sollen auch Dusche und Fernsehen haben.

Da wir tagsüber Ausflüge machen wollen, würden wir nur Frühstück und Abendessen bei Ihnen einnehmen. Um wieviel Uhr sind eigentlich Frühstück und Abendessen?

Laut Ortsplan befindet sich Gasthof Lehen ziemlich weit außerhalb des Ortes. Könnten Sie mir deshalb Auskunft über Busverbindungen zwischen Lehen und Telfs senden?

Könnten Sie bitte diese Reservierung sobald wie möglich bestätigen und die Preise für Halbpension inklusive Bedienung angeben? Falls der Gasthof für diese Zeit voll belegt ist, würden Sie mir einen anderen Gasthof in der Nähe empfehlen?

Hochachtungsvoll
Peter Williams

[157 words]

A Write a letter of about 150 words to a hotel in which you:

1. State in which month and with whom you will be coming

2. Give the exact dates of arrival and departure

3. Ask for the particular room(s) you require

4. State the features you want the room(s) to have

5. Say whether you want full or half board

6. Ask what times meals are served

7. Ask about services linking the hotel to other places

8. Ask for confirmation of your booking

9. Ask for information about prices

10. Request that another hotel be recommended to you should this one be fully booked for the period you require

In this letter, try particularly to:

✱ use subordinate clauses with *da, wenn* and *falls* (as in the model letter).

✱ use the conditional tense.

✱ use all four cases.

B Imagine you are the manager(ess) of the hotel. Reply to Peter Williams' letter in about 150 words. Include the following points:

1. Thank Mr Williams for his letter. The hotel is not fully booked, and the reservation is confirmed

2. The rooms have a balcony with a view of the mountains, and a shower and T.V. as requested

3. Breakfast is served between 7 a.m. and 9 a.m., evening dinner between 6 p.m. and 8 p.m.

4. The price for half board is 200 Austrian Schillings per day for adults, 150 per day for the children

5. There is a regular bus service between Gasthof Lehen and Telfs. A timetable is enclosed

6. You are looking forward to meeting Mr Williams and his family

In this letter, try particularly to:

✱ use all four cases

✱ use two subordinate clauses preceding a main clause (as in the model letter).

✱ use the particles *wohl* and *ja* (Language Resource Bank, section B.2).

Cardiff, den 18. August

Berggasthof Lehen
Lehen 3
A-6410 Telfs/Tirol

Liebe Frau Hellrigl,

zuerst bedanke ich mich herzlich bei Ihnen für Ihre Gastfreundschaft und Ihr Entgegenkommen während unseres Aufenthalts in Telfs. Wir werden unsere Zeit bei Ihnen noch lange in bester Erinnerung behalten.

Ich hätte jetzt eine Bitte an Sie. Kurz nach unserer Ankunft hier zuhause ist mir eingefallen, daß ich ein Buch im Nachttisch neben meinem Bett vergessen habe. Es ist ein Führer für Österreich, den ich in Innsbruck gekauft habe. Da ich bestimmt wieder nach Österreich komme, will ich das Buch nicht verlieren, und ich bitte Sie daher, es mir nachzusenden. Selbstverständlich bezahle ich das Porto nach Großbritannien.

Auch haben wir entdeckt, daß unser Sohn ein Abzeichen mit der olympischen Sprungschanze darauf entweder vergessen oder verloren hat. Würden Sie so gut sein und im Gasthof nachsehen, ob er es liegenlassen hat? Sollte es zum Vorschein kommen, bitte senden Sie es mit dem Buch nach.

Nochmals herzlichen Dank für alles.
              Mit freundlichem Gruß
              Ihr
              Peter Williams

[153 words]

A On your return home from a holiday in Germany, you discover that you have left something behind in the hotel. Write to the hotel manager(ess) in about 150 words and include the following:

1. Who you are and when you stayed in the hotel

2. What you have forgotten

3. A brief description of the item

4. Where you think you may have left it

5. Would the manager(ess) be kind enough to look for it if it is not in the place mentioned?

6. Ask if it could be sent to you

7. Say you will pay the postage

8. Thank the manager(ess) for his/her trouble

In this letter, try particularly to:

* use the conditional tense.

* use subordinate clauses with *daß* and *ob* (as in the model letter).

* use all four cases.

B Imagine you are the hotel manager(ess) replying to the letter. In about 150 words, tell Mr Williams:

1. That you are pleased he and his family enjoyed their stay

2. That the book was discovered in the bedside locker the day after they had left

3. That the badge had been found in the recreation room (Aufenthalt-sraum)

4. That it would be sent separately (getrennt)

5. That the hotel is quite happy to pay the postage for the two items

6. That you hope you will have the pleasure of welcoming him and his family again

In this letter, try particularly to:

* use the pluperfect tense.

* use the future tense.

* use subordinate clauses with *nachdem* and *daß*.

Part Four
LANGUAGE RESOURCE BANK

6

Language Resource Bank

INTRODUCTORY NOTE — It is not intended that the vocabulary listed in this chapter should be learned by heart. You should use this section rather like a dictionary, i.e. it should be dipped into and words selected for inclusion in compositions as required. As the vocabulary has been grouped according to theme, you should find it easy to find useful expressions quite quickly.

A   USEFUL GENERAL VOCABULARY

A1

1) SETTING THE SCENE

i) WANN ?

am Abend	*in the evening*
am letzten Freitag	*last Friday*
am letzten Tag	*on the last day*
am Morgen	*in the morning*
am Nachmittag	*in the afternoon*
an einem herrlichen Julimorgen	*on a lovely morning in July*
eines Abends	*one evening*
eines Morgens	*one morning*
eines Nachmittags	*one afternoon*
eines Nachts	*one night*
eines Sommermorgens	*one summer morning*
eines Tages	*one day*
früh am Tage	*early in the day*
frühmorgens	*early in the morning*
gestern morgen	*yesterday morning*
gestern vormittag	*yesterday morning*
gestern mittag	*yesterday at noon*
gestern abend	*yesterday evening*
im Frühjahr	*early in the year*
im Frühsommer	*early in the summer*
im Laufe des Tages	*in the course of the day*
im tiefsten Winter	*in the heart of winter*
letzte Woche	*last week*
letzten Dienstag	*last Tuesday*

102

letzten Juli	*last July*
letzten Monat	*last month*
letztes Jahr	*last year*
spät am Abend	*late in the evening*
spät am Tag	*late in the day*
um die Mittagsstunde	*at noon*
vor einem Jahr	*a year ago*
vor einem Monat	*a month ago*
während der Sommerferien	*during the summer holidays*
zu Ostern	*at Easter*
zu Pfingsten	*at Whitsun*
zu Weihnachten	*at Christmas*

ii) WER ?

der Bauer	*farmer, peasant*
der Beamte	*official*
die Beamtin	
der/die Bekannte	*acquaintance*
der Bergsteiger	*climber*
der Besucher	*visitor*
der Bewohner	*occupant*
der Bursche	*lad*
das Ehepaar	*married couple*
der Fahrgast	*passenger, (bus, taxi)*
der/die Fremde	*stranger*
der Fußgänger	*pedestrian*
der/die Jugendliche	*young person, teenager*
der Kamerad	*friend, companion*
die Kameradin	
der Kerl	*chap, fellow*
ein komischer Kauz	*an odd character*
der Kollege	*colleague*
die Kollegin	
der Kumpel	*pal*
der Passagier	*passenger (plane, ship)*
der/die Reisende	*passenger (train)*
der Schwimmer	*swimmer*
der Spaziergänger	*walker, stroller*
der Wanderer	*hiker*
der Witzbold	*practical joker*

iii) WO ?

auf dem Bahnhof	*at the station*
auf dem Bahnsteig	*on the platform*
auf dem Bauernhof	*on the farm*
in den Bergen	*in the mountains*
im Büro	*in the office*
auf dem Campingplatz	*at the campsite*
im Feld	*in the field*
auf einem Felsen	*on a rock*
auf dem Flughafen	*at the airport*
am Fluß	*by the river*
im Freien	*in the open*
am Fuß eines Berg(e)s	*at the foot of a mountain*
im Garten	*in the garden*

auf dem Gipfel	*on the summit*
im Hafen	*in the port*
an der Kasse	*at the till*
im Kino	*in the cinema*
auf den Klippen	*on the cliffs*
in der Kirche	*in the church*
in der Küche	*in the kitchen*
im Laden	*in the shop*
auf dem Land	*in the country*
aufs Land	*to the country*
auf einer Landstraße	*on a country road*
auf dem Marktplatz	*at the market*
am Meer	*by the sea*
auf dem Platz	*in the square*
auf dem Postamt	*at the post office*
auf dem Schiff	*on the ship*
im Schlafzimmer	*in the bedroom*
im Schiff	*in the ship*
im Schwimmbad	*in the swimming pool*
am See	*by the lake*
an der See	*at the seaside*
in der Stadt	*in the town*
in der Stadtmitte	*in the town centre*
am Strand	*on the beach*
auf der Straße	*in the street*
im Tal	*in the valley*
an der Tankstelle	*at the petrol station*
am Ufer eines Flusses	*on the bank of a river*
im Wald	*in the wood*
im Warenhaus	*in the department store*
auf der Wiese	*in the meadow*
im Wohnzimmer	*in the living room*
im Zug	*in the train*

2) FEELINGS AND REACTIONS

In addition to the expressions below see also section B.1 (*glücklich, unglücklich, zornig*) and the appropriate idiom categories in section C.

große Angst haben	*to be very frightened*
sich ärgern über (+ acc)	*to get angry at/about*
den Atem anhalten	*to hold one's breath*
erleichtert auf/atmen	*to sigh with relief*
sich auf/regen	*to get excited*
jemanden beruhigen	*to calm someone*
jemanden beunruhigen	*to alarm/disturb someone*
eifersüchtig [neidisch] (auf + acc) sein	*to be jealous [envious] (of)*
sich freuen auf (+ acc)	*to look forward to*
sich freuen über (+ acc)	*to be pleased about*
sich fühlen	*to feel*
gefallen (es gefällt + dat)	*to like*
gefesselt stehen/bleiben	*to stop in amazement*
in Gelächter [Tränen] aus/brechen	*to burst out laughing [into tears]*
hilflos da/stehen	*to stand helplessly*
juchzen	*to shriek with delight*

sich langweilen	to be bored
gute [schlechte] Laune haben	to be in a good [bad] mood
vor Scham [Verlegenheit] erröten (*with* sein)	to blush with shame [embarrassment]
sich schämen (wegen + *genitive*)	to be ashamed (of)
vor Angst [Schmerz]/[Wut] schreien	to scream with fear [pain]/[rage]
staunen (über + *acc*)	to be amazed/astonished (at)
jemanden in fröhliche Stimmung versetzen	to put someone in a cheerful mood
stolz sein (auf + *acc*)	to be proud (of)
zu Tode erschrecken (*with* sein)	to be frightened to death
jemanden in Wut versetzen	to send someone into a rage
vor Angst [Aufregung]/[Kälte] zittern	to shiver with fear [excitement]/[cold]
in Zorn geraten (*with* sein)	to lose one's temper

(A2)

3) EXCLAMATIONS

A3

Abgemacht!	Agreed! O.K.! That's settled!
Ach du liebe Güte!	Oh my goodness! Goodness me!
Alles Gute!	All the best!
Ausgeschlossen!	Out of the question! No way!
Bravo!	Well done!
Dalli, dalli!	Get a move on!
So was Dummes!	How stupid!
Einverstanden!	Agreed! O.K.!
Entschuldigung!	I'm sorry! Excuse me!
Entsetzlich!	Awful! Terrible!
Gott sei Dank!	Thank God!
Guten Appetit!	Enjoy your meal!
Gute Reise!	A pleasant journey!
Hals- und Beinbruch!	Good luck!
Hör auf!	Stop it!
Ich gratuliere!	Congratulations!
Komm mal her!	Come here a minute!
Köstlich!	Priceless! (of humour)
Das setzt allem die Krone auf!	That's the last straw!
Leise!	Quietly!
Mensch!	(Oh) boy! Wow!
(So ein) Mist!	Blast!
Moment mal!	Hold it!
Prima!	Great!
Prost!	Cheers! (Good health!)
Quatsch!	Nonsense! Rubbish!
Scher dich!	Beat it!
Schon gut!	O.K.! Fine!
Das ist doch eine Schweinerei!	That's a dirty trick!
Das ist aber toll!	That's really terrific!
Tschüß!	Bye!
Unglaublich!	Unbelievable!
Das ist ja unverschämt!	Of all the cheek!
Verflixt nochmal!	Blow!
Viel Spaß!	Have a good time!
Vorsicht!	Careful!
Na, so was!	Well I never!
Was soll denn das?	What's all this, then?
Wie schade!	What a pity!
Wie schön!	How nice!

4) ACTIVITY, BEHAVIOUR

sich amüsieren	to enjoy oneself
an/fangen, etwas zu tun	to begin/start doing something
jemanden an/starren	to stare at someone
sich an/strengen, etwas zu tun	to make an effort to do something
sich an die Arbeit machen	to get down to work
sich über etwas (*acc*) ärgern	to be annoyed at something
auf/fahren (*with* sein)	to start with surprise
sich auf/raffen, etwas zu tun	to rouse oneself to do something
sich auf/richten	to sit up straight
aus/rutschen (*with* sein)	to slip
auf/stehen (*with* sein)	to get/stand up
auf/wachen (*with* sein)	to wake up
sich beeilen	to hurry up, to get a move on
sich bemühen, etwas zu tun	to try hard to do something
beobachten	to observe closely, to watch
sich beschäftigen mit	to busy/occupy oneself with
beschließen	to decide
das Bewußtsein verlieren	to lose consciousness
wieder zu Bewußtsein kommen	to regain consciousness
davon/laufen (*with* sein)	to run away
eilen	to hurry
entdecken	to discover
entscheiden	to decide
ergreifen	to seize
fallen (*with* sein)	to fall
fangen	to catch
fort/gehen (*with* sein)	to go away, to go off
fort/laufen (*with* sein)	to run off
sich fühlen	to feel
sich fürchten (vor + *dat*)	to be afraid (of)
das Gleichgewicht verlieren	to lose one's balance
halten	to stop
hinauf/gehen (*with* sein)	to go up
hinaus/gehen (*with* sein)	to go out
hinein/gehen (*with* sein)	to go in
hinüber/gehen	to go across
hinunter/gehen (*with* sein)	to go down
klettern (auf + *acc*)	to climb (up)
jemanden ins Krankenhaus bringen	to take someone to hospital
kriechen (*with* sein)	to creep, crawl
lächeln	to smile
lachen	to laugh
laufen (*with* sein)	to run
jemandem nach/laufen (*with* sein)	to chase someone
jemandem nach/rufen	to call after someone
schlendern (*with* sein)	to stroll
schleppen	to drag
schütteln	to shake
sich setzen	to sit down
spazieren/gehen (*with* sein)	to go for a walk
springen (*with* sein)	to jump
spüren	to sense
stehen/bleiben (*with* sein)	to stop

steigen (*with* sein)	to climb
suchen	to look for, to search
sich um/drehen	to turn round
sich verirren	to get lost, to lose one's way
verletzen	to injure
verschwinden	to disappear
sich verspäten	to be late
sich verstecken	to hide
versuchen	to try
an jemandem vorbei/gehen	to go past someone
wandern (*with* sein)	to hike, to ramble
sich auf den Weg machen	to set off
weg/gehen (*with* sein)	to go away, to go off
weinen	to cry
weiter/gehen (*with* sein)	to continue walking, to go on
werfen	to throw
ziehen	to pull
zögern	to hesitate
auf jemanden zu/gehen (*with* sein)	to go up to someone
auf jemanden zu/kommen (*with* sein)	to come up to someone
jemandem zu/lächeln	to smile at someone
jemandem zu/rufen	to call to someone
zurück/gehen (*with* sein)	to go back
jemandem zuwinken	to wave to someone

5) SCHLUß (CONCLUSION, OUTCOME)

mit einem blauen Auge davon/kommen	to get off lightly
Seine Bemühungen waren ohne Erfolg	His efforts were unsuccessful
Ende gut, alles gut	All's well that ends well
Das Ende vom Lied war, daß . . .	The (sad) end of the story was that . . .
Das dicke Ende kam noch	The worst was yet to come
Es hat alles einmal ein Ende	Everything must come to an end
etwas zu einem guten Ende bringen	to bring something to a satisfactory conclusion
Diese Geschichte nimmt ein böses [glückliches] Ende	This story has an unhappy [happy] ending
aus Erfahrung lernen	to learn from experience
ein günstiges Ergebnis	a favourable outcome
Die Folge war, daß . . .	The result was that . . .
etwas ohne Rücksicht auf die Folgen tun	to do something regardless of the outcome
aus dem gröbsten heraus sein	to be over the worst
dabei wird nichts Gutes heraus/kommen	no good will come out of it
mit heiler Haut davon/kommen	to escape unhurt
es stellte sich heraus, daß . . .	it turned out that
auf eine gute Idee kommen	to have a good idea
Wer zuletzt lacht, lacht am besten	He who laughs last laughs longest
Lehrgeld zahlen	to learn things the hard way
Es hatte sich nicht gelohnt	It had not been worth the trouble
Das war das erste und bis jetzt das letzte Mal, daß . . .	this was the first and the last time that . . .
mit knapper Not davon/kommen	to escape by the skin of one's teeth
Das Schlimmste war, daß . . .	The worst thing of all was that . . .
Das war alles umsonst	It was all in vain

6) TIME LINKS AND EXPLANATION LINKS

To ensure that your compositions flow smoothly and that the content is logical to follow, you should establish clear links between events. The following vocabulary items will help you to do this.

i. Time links

auf einmal	*all of a sudden*
bald danach	*soon after*
einige Wochen vergingen	*a few weeks passed*
einige Minuten später	*a few minutes later*
endlich/schließlich	*finally*
erst dann	*only then*
Es dauerte einige Zeit, bis . . .	*It took some time until . . .*
Es entstand eine kurze Pause. Dann . . .	*There was a short pause. Then . . .*
Es war schon zwei Uhr, als . . .	*It was already 2 o'clock when . . .*
Es wurde endlich Zeit, . . . zu . . .	*It was finally time to . . .*
etwas später	*a little later*
früh am nächsten Morgen	*early next morning*
Gerade als ich gehen wollte . . .	*Just as I was about to go*
gerade in dem Augenblick	*at that very moment*
im Nu	*in a flash, in the twinkling of an eye*
in der nächsten Sekunde	*the very next moment*
In kurzer Zeit gelang es ihm . . .	*In a short time he managed . . .*
inzwischen	*meanwhile*
kurz darauf	*shortly after*
nach dem Essen	*after the meal*
nach zweistündiger Fahrt	*after a two hour journey/drive*
nach diesen Worten	*after saying this*
nach mehreren Wochen	*after several weeks*
ohne einen Augenblick zu verlieren	*without wasting a moment's time*
ohne lange zu zögern	*without much hesitation*
plötzlich	*suddenly*
seit diesem Tag	*ever since that day*
später am Abend	*later in the evening*
unterwegs	*on the way*

ii. Explanation links

The best way of showing the connections between different events and circumstances is to use 'subordinating conjunctions' (words like 'because', 'since', 'while' etc. used at the beginning of a clause). The examples below show how they are used.

als = **when**   *Als er die stürmische See sah, zitterte der Passagier vor Angst.*   When he saw the stormy sea the passenger shivered with fear.

_da_ = **since, as**   *Da wir kein Geld hatten, mußten wir zu Hause bleiben.*   As we had no money we had to stay at home.

nachdem = **after**   *Nachdem er seine Badehose angezogen hatte, sprang er ins Wasser.*   After he had put on his swimming trunks he dived into the water.

während = **while** *Während Helmut seine Hausaufgaben machte, sah sein Bruder fern.* While Helmut was doing his homework his brother watched T.V.

weil = **because** *Weil ich mich verschlafen hatte, kam ich zu spät.* Because I had overslept I was late.

Two further useful expressions are *kaum* and *um . . . zu:*

kaum = **hardly** *Ich war kaum im Garten, als es zu regnen begann.* Hardly had I gone into the garden when it began to rain.

um . . . zu = **(in order) to** *Wir fuhren nach Bonn, um das Beethovenhaus zu sehen.* We travelled to Bonn (in order) to see Beethoven's house.

B │ SYNONYMS AND SOME COMMON PARTICLES

1) SYNONYMS

There are certain German words that are regularly over-used in examination essays: these include such common adjectives as *gut, schlecht, groß* and *klein*. We can also add to the list the most overworked words for expressing feelings and reactions: *glücklich* and *unglücklich*. To help you enrich your vocabulary, here is a list of alternatives to some of the words that tend to be over-used.

i) Groß

gewaltig	*colossal, immense (e.g. buildings, mountains, efforts)*
gigantisch	*colossal, gigantic (e.g. buildings, mountains, person)*
katastrophal	*catastrophic, disastrous (e.g. effects of a natural disaster)*
mächtig	*mighty (e.g. mountains, rocks, trees)*
riesig	*gigantic, huge (e.g. buildings, mountains, persons)*
ungeheuer	*enormous, immense (e.g. distance, height, size, pains)*
wuchtig	*massive (big and heavy, as a tree for example)*

ii) Klein

gering	*low, slight (e.g. chance, talent)*
geringfügig	*minor, slight (e.g. injury, loss)*
kleinlich	*petty (e.g. person)*
winzig	*tiny (e.g. animal, building)*
zierlich	*dainty, petite (e.g. figure, hands, woman)*

iii) Gut

angenehm	*pleasant (e.g. person, journey, surprise, smell)*
ausgezeichnet	*excellent (e.g. doctor, driver, skier, meal, film)*
eindrucksvoll	*impressive (e.g. speech, personality)*
entzückend	*delightful (e.g. dress, picture, landscape)*
fabelhaft	*fabulous (e.g. fellow, singer, drink)*
großartig	*great (e.g. cook, wine, idea, achievement)*
herrlich	*glorious (e.g. weather, day, view)*
hervorragend	*outstanding (e.g. actor, meal, wine, achievement)*
imponierend	*impressive (e.g. person, attitude, knowledge)*

imposant	imposing (e.g. physique, building, work of art)
lobenswert	praiseworthy (e.g. behaviour, work)
prächtig	magnificent (e.g. person, weather, city, work, achievement)
reizend	charming (e.g. child, girl, face, place, picture)
vorzüglich	superb (e.g. speaker, actor, meal)

iv) Schlecht

ekelhaft	disgusting (e.g. behaviour, weather)
entsetzlich	hideous (e.g. crime, sight)
erbärmlich	pitiful, wretched (e.g. speech, achievement)
furchtbar	awful (e.g. person, sight, illness, pain, crime, storm)
gemein	mean, nasty (e.g. person, face, laugh, lie)
gräßlich	horrible (e.g. accident, sight, weather, a cold)
jämmerlich	deplorable, lamentable, (e.g. explanation, excuse)
kläglich	pathetic, wretched (e.g. achievement, end, defeat)
nichtswürdig	despicable, worthless (e.g. person)
scheußlich	dreadful (e.g. sight, weather, crime, building)
schrecklich	terrible (e.g. person, mood, noise, fear, news, heat/cold, surprise, illness, experience)
schlimm	bad, naughty (e.g. person, thought, mistake, situation)
übel	evil, wicked (e.g. person, company, reputation)
unverbesserlich	incorrigible (e.g. person, optimist)
verächtlich	contemptuous (e.g. manner, look, laugh, words)

v) Glücklich

amüsiert	amused
begeistert	enthusiastic
entzückt	delighted
freudig	joyful
froh	happy
fröhlich	cheerful
lustig	merry
überglücklich	overjoyed
vergnügt	pleased
verzückt	ecstatic
zufrieden	content

vi) Unglücklich

ängstlich	anxious
besorgt	worried
deprimiert	depressed
enttäuscht	disappointed
jämmerlich	pitiful
niedergeschlagen	dejected
unzufrieden	dissatisfied
verlegen	embarrassed
verwirrt	confused
verzagt	disheartened, despondent
verzweifelt	desperate

vii) Zornig

ärgerlich	annoyed	grimmig	enraged
böse	cross	rasend	livid
empört	indignant, disgusted	verärgert	angry, annoyed
entsetzt	appalled	wild	wild
frostig	frosty	wütend	furious

viii) Sagen

antworten	to answer	hinzu/fügen	to add
befehlen	to order	klagen	to complain
behaupten	to maintain	knurren	to growl
entgegnen	to retort	rufen	to call
erklären	to explain	schimpfen	to grumble
erwidern	to reply	schreien	to scream
fort/fahren	to continue	seufzen	to sigh
hervor/stoßen	to gasp	vor/werfen	to reproach

ix) The Unusual

As "something out of the ordinary" crops up in a large number of essays set for examinations, it may be helpful to know some adjectives that express the unusual.

außerordentlich	*out of the ordinary*
erstaunlich	*astonishing*
lächerlich	*ridiculous*
merkwürdig	*odd*
seltsam	*strange*
sonderbar	*peculiar*
überraschend	*surprising*
unerwartet	*unexpected*
ungewöhnlich	*unusual*
verblüffend	*amazing*

2) SOME COMMON PARTICLES

There is a small group of words, called particles, that are used idiomatically a very great deal. They are often difficult to translate, because each one has various shades of meaning. If you learn to use them correctly, they will greatly enhance the quality of your written style by making it read more like authentic, everyday German.

You will find 9 particles listed below. For each particle, various shades of meaning are given with examples of use in a German phrase or sentence followed by an English translation. (The more obvious meanings, e.g. ja = yes, have been omitted.)

1) DOCH

a) For emphasis

Das weißt du doch.	*But you <u>know</u> that.*
Komm doch!	*Come on!*
Schrei doch nicht!	*Stop shouting!*
Du kommst doch?	*You <u>are</u> coming?*

b) Yet

Dieses Tier ist schön, doch gefährlich.	*This animal is beautiful yet dangerous*
Ich habe ihm drei Briefe geschrieben, doch keine Antwort bekommen.	*I have written him three letters yet I have received no answer.*

c) Yes (as a contradiction)

Du willst nicht mitkommen? – Doch!	*Don't you want to come? – Yes, I do!*

d) Really, after all, in the end

Du hast den Brief doch geschrieben.	*So you wrote the letter after all.*
Es ist doch so, wie ich es mir vorgestellt habe.	*It really is just as I imagined.*

111

e) **But** (as emphasis)

Das ist doch gar nicht wahr.	*But that just isn't true.*
Das ist doch die Höhe!	*But/well that's the limit!*

f) **Assuming knowledge** (on someone else's part)

Du weißt doch, wie alt sie ist?	*You know how old she is, don't you?*
Hier darf man doch nicht angeln.	*You can't fish here you know.*
Du sprichst doch Deutsch. Wie sagt man . . .?	*But you speak German. How does one say . . .?*

ii) EBEN

a) **Just, simply**

Dann gehst du eben allein.	*Then you'll just have to go alone.*
Du hättest es ihm eben nicht sagen sollen.	*You just shouldn't have told him.*

b) **The immediate past**

Was hat er eben gesagt?	*What was it he just said?*
Sie war eben drüben im Geschäft.	*She was only just in the shop over there.*

c) **In/For a short while**

Ich gehe eben zum Zeitungskiosk.	*I'll just pop over to the newspaper kiosk.*
Kommst du eben mit?	*Will you come with me for a minute?*

d) **Exactly**

Das ist es eben!/Na eben!	*That's just it!/Precisely!*
Eben das wollte ich sagen.	*That's just what I wanted to say.*
Nicht eben billig [schön].	*Not exactly cheap [beautiful].*

e) **Only just**

Mit diesem Geld komme ich eben aus.	*I can just manage on this money.*
Ich habe den Zug eben noch erreicht.	*I only just caught the train.*

iii) ETWA

a) **Approximately, about**

Wir landen in etwa zehn Minuten.	*We'll be landing in about ten minutes.*
Der Berg ist etwa tausend Meter hoch.	*The mountain is about 1000 metres high.*
So etwa geht es auch.	*It's possible in roughly that way too.*

b) **For example**

Slawische Länder, wie etwa Polen und Rußland	*Slavonic countries, as for example Poland and Russia.*
Wenn du etwa zu Fuß gehst . . .	*If you go on foot, for example . . .*

c) **Perhaps**

Ist dir etwa kalt?	*Are you perhaps cold?*
Hast du etwa meinen Bruder gesehen?	*Have you by any chance seen my brother?*

iv) JA

a) For emphasis

Das weißt du ja.	*But of course you <u>know</u> that.*
Das ist ja ärgerlich.	*That's really annoying.*

b) In commands (to drive the point home)

Vergiß ja nicht!	*Don't forget!*
Schrei ja nicht!	*Stop shouting!*

c) After all (making allowances)

Er ist ja zum ersten Mal hier.	*It's his first time here, after all.*
Es ist ja erst zehn Uhr.	*It's only 10 o'clock, after all.*

d) Matters of fact

Sie ist ja ganz nett.	*She really is quite nice.*
Es regnet ja.	*Look, it's raining.*

v) MAL

The colloquial form of **einmal**

a) A point in time (past or future)

Komm mich mal besuchen.	*Come and visit me sometime.*
Du wirst es mal bereuen.	*You'll regret it one day.*
Warst du schon mal in Wien?	*Have you ever been to Vienna?*

b) Emphasising requests

Laß mich mal sehen.	*Let me see.*
Sprich mal Deutsch.	*Go on, speak German.*

vi) NUR

a) Just (in commands)

Laß das nur!	*Just leave off!*
Geh nur!	*Just go/go on.*

b) Negative commands (whatever you do)

Sag das nur nicht dem Lehrer.	*Don't tell the teacher, whatever you do.*
Laß es nur niemand sehen.	*Don't let anyone see it, whatever you do.*

c) Reinforcing a statement

Ich schreibe, so schnell ich nur kann.	*I'm writing just as fast as I can.*
Wie schön sie nur aussieht!	*How lovely she looks!*

d) Reinforcing <u>alles</u>

Du kannst nicht alles haben, was du nur willst.	*You can't have absolutely everything you want.*
Alles, was nur möglich ist.	*Everything that's at all possible.*

e) With interrogatives (-ever, on earth)

Was hat er nur?

Warum machst du das nur?

Whatever
What on earth   is up with him?
Whyever
Why on earth   do you do it?

vii) SCHON

a) Pinpointing time

Ich werde es dir schon sagen, wenn . . .
Er wollte schon abfahren, als . . .

Schon am nächsten Morgen.
Ich bin schon um zehn Uhr im Bett.

I'll be sure to tell you when . . .
He was just on the point of leaving,
when . . .
The very next morning.
I'm in bed by 10 o'clock.

b) Impatience

Geh schon!
Mach schon!
Ich komme schon!
Hör schon auf!

Go on!
Get a move on!
I'm coming!
Cut it out!

c) Expressing sufficiency

Schon der Gedanke macht mich wütend.
Wenn ich das schon sehe!
Das genügt schon. Mehr brauche ich nicht
zu schreiben.

Schon gut!

The very thought makes me mad.
Just the sight of it!

That's enough. I don't need to write any
more.
O.K.!

d) Being definite about something

Du wirst schon sehen.
Sie wird schon kommen.

Just you wait and see.
She'll come (you can be sure of it).

viii) SO

a) In such a way

So geht es nicht.
Du kannst es so machen.
So ist es richtig.

It can't be done like that.
You can do it like this.
That's the right way.

b) Being imprecise about something

Er kommt so um zwei Uhr.
Samstags gehe ich zuerst in die
Buchhandlung, dann gehe ich ins Café oder
ins Restaurant oder so.

He's coming at 2 o'clock or so.

Saturdays I go to the book-shop first then
perhaps I might go to the café or the
restaurant.

114

ix) WOHL

a) Supposition

Er wird wohl noch kommen.	*I expect he'll still come.*
Du willst wohl hier bleiben?	*I presume you want to stay here?*
Es wird wohl noch zwei Stunden dauern, bis . . .	*It will presumably/I suppose take another two hours until . . .*
Wo sind wir wohl jetzt?	*Where do you suppose we are now?*

b) Indeed, certainly

Das hat er wohl gesagt, aber ich glaube ihm nicht.	*He did indeed say that but I don't believe him.*
Es kann wohl mal passieren, daß . . .	*It might well happen that . . .*

C | USEFUL IDIOMS

For a wider range of idioms, with examples of use, see Everyday German Idioms *by J.P. Lupson (also published by Stanley Thornes).*

The careful use of idioms can do much to add to the quality and naturalness of your style – but be careful not to overdo it! Only include idioms at points where they offer a particularly neat way of putting across somebody's way of seeing things.

For convenience, the idioms listed below have been presented in distinct categories. If for instance, you are required to write an essay or letter reporting a dangerous situation, you can consult the section called 'Difficulties, danger' and select an idiom to fit this kind of situation. You could also include an idiom from a related section such as 'Despair' or 'Fear', to heighten the atmosphere.

1) Despair

ANGST	in tausend Ängsten schweben	*to be frantic*
FLINTE	die Flinte ins Korn werfen	*to give up, throw in the towel*
KOPF	den Kopf verlieren	*to lose one's head*
KOPF	die Hände über dem Kopf zusammenschlagen	*to throw up one's hands in horror*
RAT	nun ist guter Rat teuer	*to be at one's wits' end*

2) Difficulties, danger

FADEN	an einem seidenen Faden hängen	*to hang by a thread (life etc.)*

115

HAKEN	die Sache hat einen Haken	*there's a snag*
SCHWEBEN	in Lebensgefahr schweben	*to be in danger of one's life*
TINTE	in der Tinte sitzen	*to be in a tight spot*
UNGLÜCK	ein Unglück kommt selten allein	*it never rains but it pours*

3) Disapproval, displeasure

GEDULD	ihm/ihr reißt die Geduld	*his/her patience is wearing thin*
GESICHT	ein langes Gesicht machen	*one's face drops*
LUFT	in die Luft gehen	*to hit the roof*
NASE	von etwas die Nase voll haben	*to be sick of something*
NERV	jemandem auf die Nerven gehen	*to get on someone's nerves*

4) Fear

FUSS	kalte Füße bekommen	*to get cold feet*
HAAR	ihm/ihr stehen die Haare zu Berge	*his/her hair stands on end*
HERZ	ihm/ihr fällt das Herz in die Hose	*his/her heart sinks into his/her boots*
RÜCKEN	es läuft einem kalt über den Rücken	*a shiver runs down someone's spine*

5) Happiness, pleasure

ELEMENT	in seinem Element sein	*to be in one's element*
HÄUSCHEN	vor Freude aus dem Häuschen sein	*to be beside oneself with joy*
HIMMEL	wie im siebten Himmel sein	*to be over the moon*
MURMELTIER	wie ein Murmeltier schlafen	*to sleep like a log*

6) Humour, ridicule

ARM	jemanden auf den Arm nehmen	*to pull someone's leg*
BILD	ein Bild für Götter sein	*to be a proper sight*
GESICHT	jemandem ein Gesicht schneiden	*to pull a face at someone*
LACHEN	da gibt es nichts zu lachen	*it's no laughing matter*
LUSTIG	sich über jemanden lustig machen	*to make fun of someone*
NARR	jemanden zum Narren halten	*to make a fool of someone*
SCHABERNACK	mit jemandem Schabernack treiben	*to play a practical joke on someone*
SCHREIEN	etwas ist zum Schreien	*something is too funny for words*

7) Rebukes

C7

MARSCH	jemandem den Marsch blasen	*to give someone a rocket*
REDE	jemanden zur Rede stellen	*to take someone to task*
STANDPUNKT	jemandem seinen Standpunkt klarmachen	*to give someone a piece of one's mind*

8) Surprise

C8

AUGE	große Augen machen	*to be wide-eyed*
DONNER	wie vom Donner gerührt dastehen	*to be thunderstruck*
MUND	Mund und Nase aufsperren	*to be open-mouthed*